B Twa
Mark Twain

$ 32.45

MARK TWAIN

Other Titles in the
People Who Made History Series

PEOPLE
WHO MADE
HISTORY

MARK TWAIN

Todd Howard, *Book Editor*

Daniel Leone, *President*
Bonnie Szumski, *Publisher*
Scott Barbour, *Managing Editor*
David M. Haugen, *Series Editor*

Greenhaven Press, Inc., San Diego, CA

Every effort has been made to trace the owners of copyrighted material. The articles in this volume may have been edited for content, length, and/or reading level. The titles have been changed to enhance the editorial purpose. Those interested in locating the original source will find the complete citation on the first page of each article.

Library of Congress Cataloging-in-Publication Data

Mark Twain / Todd Howard, book editor.
        p. cm. — (People who made history)
     Includes bibliographical references and index.
     ISBN 0-7377-0897-2 (lib. bdg. : alk. paper) —
ISBN 0-7377-0896-4 (pbk. : alk. paper)
     1. Twain, Mark, 1835–1910. 2. Authors, American—19th century—Biography. 3. Humorists, American—19th century—Biography. I. Howard, Todd, 1964– II. Series.

PS1331 .M218   2002
818'.409—dc21   2001028923
[B]   CIP

Cover photo: Bettmann/CORBIS
Library of Congress, 21, 47, 153
North Wind, 104

Copyright © 2002 by Greenhaven Press, Inc.
10911 Technology Place
San Diego, CA 92127
Printed in the U.S.A.

"If I'd a knowed what a trouble it was to make a book I wouldn't a tackled it and ain't agoing to no more."

—Huck Finn

CONTENTS

embrace Mark Twain's literary persona on its own terms rather than seek to unmask the Samuel Clemens behind it. Likewise, they must indulge and embrace his persona's dubious narrative subjectivity to fully appreciate its transcendent and triumphant interpretive power.

Chapter 4: Mark Twain's Legacy

FOREWORD

In the vast and colorful pageant of human history, a handful of individuals stand out. They are the men and women who have come variously to be called "great," "leading," "brilliant," "pivotal," or "infamous" because they and their deeds forever changed their own society or the world as a whole. Some were political or military leaders—kings, queens, presidents, generals, and the like—whose policies, conquests, or innovations reshaped the maps and futures of countries and entire continents. Among those falling into this category were the formidable Roman statesman/general Julius Caesar, who extended Rome's power into Gaul (what is now France); Caesar's lover and ally, the notorious Egyptian queen Cleopatra, who challenged the strongest male rulers of her day; and England's stalwart Queen Elizabeth I, whose defeat of the mighty Spanish Armada saved England from subjugation.

Some of history's other movers and shakers were scientists or other thinkers whose ideas and discoveries altered the way people conduct their everyday lives or view themselves and their place in nature. The electric light and other remarkable inventions of Thomas Edison, for example, revolutionized almost every aspect of home-life and the workplace; and the theories of naturalist Charles Darwin lit the way for biologists and other scientists in their ongoing efforts to understand the origins of living things, including human beings.

Still other people who made history were religious leaders and social reformers. The struggles of the Arabic prophet Muhammad more than a thousand years ago led to the establishment of one of the world's great religions—Islam; and the efforts and personal sacrifices of an American reverend named Martin Luther King Jr. brought about major improvements in race relations and the justice system in the United States.

Each anthology in the People Who Made History series begins with an introductory essay that provides a general overview of the individual's life, times, and contributions. The group of essays that follow are chosen for their accessibility to a young adult audience and carefully edited in consideration of the reading and comprehension levels of that audience. Some of the essays are by noted historians, professors, and other experts. Others are excerpts from contemporary writings by or about the pivotal individual in question. To aid the reader in choosing the material of immediate interest or need, an annotated table of contents summarizes the article's main themes and insights.

Each volume also contains extensive research tools, including a collection of excerpts from primary source documents pertaining to the individual under discussion. The volumes are rounded out with an extensive bibliography and a comprehensive index.

Plutarch, the renowned first-century Greek biographer and moralist, crystallized the idea behind Greenhaven's People Who Made History when he said, "To be ignorant of the lives of the most celebrated men of past ages is to continue in a state of childhood all our days." Indeed, since it is people who make history, every modern nation, organization, institution, invention, artifact, and idea is the result of the diligent efforts of one or more individuals, living or dead; and it is therefore impossible to understand how the world we live in came to be without examining the contributions of these individuals.

MARK TWAIN: AN AMERICAN STAR

Samuel Langhorne Clemens was born on November 30, 1835, in Florida, Missouri. Florida, a tiny agricultural hamlet nestled between two tributaries of the great Mississippi River, had a population of only one hundred residents when Sam was born and had been founded a mere four years prior. Sam's father, John Marshall Clemens, had moved the family to Florida from Kentucky in search of employment just months before Sam's birth. Though John was a descendent of Virginia plantation gentry, he was a never-do-well village lawyer whose endless financial schemes kept his family in a state of constant financial decline and frequent relocation. John Clemens was an emotionally aloof man, a staunch skeptic, and, in stark contrast to Sam's devout Presbyterian mother, an avowed agnostic. Jane Lampton Clemens was a distant descendent of British aristocracy. Such pedigree afforded no special privileges on the harsh American frontier, however, and life was a constant struggle for Jane, as it had been for her colonial forebearers. Supplementing Jane's Presbyterianism were the superstitions and folklore that had abounded during her youth on the Kentucky frontier. She was a firm believer that the stars, along with many other signs from nature, could foretell the future (she named Sam's older brother after the constellation Orion, under which he was born). For Jane, the fact that Sam's birth coincided with the appearance of Halley's comet was a clear sign that he was destined to lead a life of greatness. She instilled into Sam throughout his childhood the belief that his life and destiny were intertwined with that of the comet. "I came in with the Comet," he would frequently declare during adulthood, "and I shall go out with the Comet."

Confusing Jane's understanding of the comet's relevance, however, had been the fact that Sam, having been born two months premature, was a frail and sickly baby. With the

11

high mortality rate of infants on the frontier, his chances for survival seemed slim. She would later note of his infancy, "I could see no promise in him. But I felt it my duty to do the best I could. To raise him if I could."[1]

When Sam was yet a frail and sickly four-year-old, his father resettled the family yet again—this time in Hannibal, Missouri, about forty miles west of Sam's birthplace of Florida. As Sam grew more robust, he would find Hannibal, which was situated along the banks of the Mississippi, to be an endless source of adventure and entertainment. "The town and its outskirts offered a variety of opportunities for boys to entertain themselves," Mark Twain biographer Margaret Sanborn notes,

> but it was the Mississippi's infinite variety and its promise of untold adventure that cast the spell. Skiffs "borrowed" from absent owners took them to Sny Island, near the Illinois shore, where in tramping through its marshy thickets they came on the nests of grebes and rails in the midst of tall reeds, and painted turtles sunning themselves in rows on half-sunken logs. Here they angled for catfish and perch. If it was the season, they went on to the mainland and searched for pecans. It was more fun to row over to the larger Glass-cock's Island (Jackson's Island in *Tom Sawyer* and *Huckleberry Finn*), opposite the mouth of Bear Creek. There, completely free, for it was uninhabited, they would throw off all their clothes, being careful when kicking off their trousers not to lose the precious amulet of rattlesnake rattles worn about the ankle to prevent cramps in swimming.[2]

Sam would return to these carefree days spent under the river's "spell" in his most famous literary works, including *The Adventures of Mark Twain, The Adventures of Huckleberry Finn,* and *Life on the Mississippi.*

Not all of Sam's memories of Hannibal and life on the river were pleasant, however. Episodes of violence were common throughout the frontier, and Hannibal was no exception. Such topics as Indian massacres, hangings, and murders were the stuff of daily conversation in the Clemens home, and Sam himself witnessed several gruesome deeds during his childhood—perhaps most notably the murder of a defenseless slave by a ruthless slave master. Of course, the grim sight of shackled slaves was itself a near-constant along the docks of the river.

Though he had found the sight of the slave's murder disturbing, Sam had been ambivalent concerning the issue of slavery throughout his childhood, since even his own parents had possessed slaves from time to time. He would later attempt in his biography to the explain the mentality of his family and fellow townsfolk who had accepted the unconscionable institution of slavery:

> It is commonly believed that an infallible effect of slavery was to make such as lived in its midst hard hearted. I think it had no such effect—speaking in general terms. I think it stupefied everybody's humanity, as regarded the slave, but stopped there. There were no hard-hearted people in our town—I mean there were no more than would be found in any other town of the same size in any other country; and in my experience hard-hearted people are very rare everywhere.[3]

SAM'S PRINTING APPRENTICESHIP

When Sam was twelve, his father died of pneumonia, and his family was driven to the brink of poverty. In the wake of this tragedy, Sam's formal education, such as it had been, was ended, and he became a printer's apprentice (or "printer's devil," as they were called) for the local Hannibal *Gazette*. As trade apprenticeships went, the work of a printer's devil was exceptionally educational (particularly for a burgeoning writer) since it required the reading of texts on a tremendous range of subjects while setting them into type. Eventually, Sam's brother Orion started his own weekly newspaper, the *Western Union*, and Sam completed his apprenticeship with him.

Sam's work in the newspaper business inspired him to try his hand at journalism, and on November 14, 1849, his first published work—a humorous piece to which he signed the pseudonym "Devil"—appeared in the Hannibal *Western Union*. During the remaining three years of his apprenticeship, he would have humorous letters printed in numerous papers, experimenting with such pseudonyms as "W. Epaminondas Adrastus Blab," "A son of Adam," "Rambler," and "Grumbler."

After completing his printing apprenticeship in 1853 and becoming a journeyman printer at age eighteen, Clemens was able to find printing work in virtually any city or large town. Eager to explore the world beyond Hannibal, Clemens served as an itinerant printer in numerous cities, including St. Louis, New York, and Philadelphia, over a period of three years. He began to send travel letters home for Orion to publish, and he experimented with many pen names and literary personae. The popularity of these travel letters published in Hannibal and elsewhere led to his being commissioned to write a series of travel letters for the Keokuk *Daily Post.* For these letters he employed the persona of one Thomas Jefferson Snodgrass, "a rustic from Keokuk whose first visit to the metropolis of St. Louis opened the way for countless awkward situations, which included being twice removed by the police for causing a near-riot during a performance of 'Julius Caesar.' His readers were treated to details of the whole affair, as well as a synopsis of the play about 'Mr. Caesar.'"[4]

PILOTING THE RIVER

By 1856, Clemens felt an increasing desire to see the world and to expand his horizons beyond the confines of a career in printing. After reading about the lucrative coca trade in the Amazon, he decided that he would make his way there to seek his fortune. In the spring of 1857, while on a Mississippi riverboat en route to New Orleans, where he intended to seek passage to South America, Clemens observed captain Horace Bixby at the ship's wheel and immediately decided that he wanted to be a riverboat pilot. Though perhaps impulsive, it was a natural career choice for one who had spent his entire life on the river and who had even once stowed away on a riverboat at age nine.

Clemens quickly convinced Bixby to take him on as an apprentice riverboat pilot, and he began an intensive tutorship under Bixby on that very day. If his printing apprenticeship had substituted for high school, then his piloting apprenticeship had served, he would later suggest, as his college education. Years later he would say that the experience of being a pilot's apprentice had been "a labor compared with which the efforts needed to acquire the degree of Doctor of Philosophy at a university are as light as a summer course of modern novels."[5] In June 1858, satisfied that he had taught Clemens all that he could, Bixby placed Clemens under the tutorship of William Brown, a master pilot and petty tyrant on the steamboat *Pennsylvania*, in order to provide Clemens with another pilot's perspective on the river.

Clemens, in turn, got his younger brother Henry work on the *Pennsylvania*. Once, when Brown had became physically abusive with Henry, Sam beat Brown into submission with a chair (while the *Pennsylvania* steamed on without a pilot), and Sam was transferred by Bixby to another steamboat as a result. A few days later, Brown's reckless participation in a boat race led to the explosion of the *Pennsylvania's* four boilers in Memphis, Tennessee, causing hundreds of people to die instantly from the explosion, and others, including Henry, to die as a result of their injuries in the days and weeks that followed. "A local newspaper reporter was present when Sam rushed into the Memphis Exchange," notes Twain biographer Ron Powers. "His account of Sam's reaction told of the depths of agony beneath that terse information":

> We witnessed one of the most affecting scenes at the Exchange yesterday that has ever been seen. The brother of Mr. Henry Clemens, second clerk of the *Pennsylvania*, who now lies dangerously ill from the injuries received by the explosion of that boat, arrived in the city yesterday afternoon, on the steamer AT Lacy [sic]. He hurried to the Exchange to see his brother, and on approaching the bedside of the wounded man, his feelings so much overcame him, at the scalded and emaciated form before him, that he sunk to the floor overpowered. There was scarcely a dry eye in the house; the poor sufferers shed tears at the sight. This brother had been pilot on the *Pennsylvania*, but fortunately for him, had remained in New Orleans when the boat started up.[6]

Though anguished and guilt-stricken over Henry's death, in September 1858, Samuel Clemens passed his licensing examination and began a brief piloting career on the Mississippi. He traveled principally between St. Louis and New Orleans until May 1861, when the escalating Civil War brought a halt to all steamboat travel on the river.

Upon returning to Hannibal, Clemens joined a group of about fifteen young men who were forming an army troop that called itself "the Marion Rangers" to aid the Confederate effort in the Civil War. Untrained, and lacking discipline and resolve, the men wandered the Missouri countryside for around two weeks, then disbanded when the prospect of engaging with Union troops presented itself. Though it is sometimes suggested that Sam was a Confederate deserter, Twain biographer Everett Emerson notes that "this service was too informal and irregular for it to be said that he was a deserter."[7]

THE NEVADA TERRITORY

Upon returning to Hannibal, Sam decided to accompany his brother Orion to the Nevada Territory. The territory was undergoing a wave of migration and settlement because of an immense vein of gold and silver that was discovered to run beneath its parched sands, and Orion had been appointed as secretary of the suddenly bustling territory for having been a strong supporter of the Abraham Lincoln presidential campaign. Sam and Orion boarded a stagecoach in St. Joseph, Missouri, bound for the Nevada Territory, and arrived nearly three weeks later, sore to the bone and filthy, in Virginia City.

Though he had accompanied Orion to serve as his assistant, Sam was not for long able to resist the call of riches and adventure, and he soon found himself amid the scorched desert on an uncooperative donkey. He continued his grueling, full-time prospecting efforts for nearly a year, but, as with the vast majority of those who had sought their fortune in the sands of the Nevada Territory, Clemens failed altogether as a prospector. Throughout this year, however, he had also been submitting humorous letters about his fruitless mining efforts to the Virginia City *Territorial Enterprise* under the pseudonym "Josh." In September 1862, Clemens accepted an offer to become a full-time reporter for the *Enterprise.*

A few months later, Clemens would first sign the pseudonym "Mark Twain" to one of his humorous travel letters. His explanation for the origins of the name was that it was a term used in steamboating to report that the river's depth was twelve feet. A depth of "mark twain" could come as either good news or bad for a pilot; if his steamboat was moving out of the shallows, the term would mean that he was entering water of safe depth. If, however, the boat was progressing into more shallow water, he was in real danger of running aground. Though it does seem likely that Clemens would have favored such a paradoxical term for his pseudonym, an alternate explanation for the origins of the nom de plume was offered in the Nevada *Sentinel*, on May 8, 1877, by the paper's editor. "We knew Clemens in the early days," he said,

> and know . . . how he came to be dubbed "Mark Twain." John Piper's Saloon . . . used to be the grand rendezvous for all . . . Virginia City Bohemians. Piper conducted a cash business, and refused to keep any books. As a special favor . . . he would occasionally chalk down drinks to the boys on the wall back of the bar. Sam Clemens, when localizing for the *Enterprise*, always had an account with the balance against him. Clemens was by no means a [spendthrift], he drank for the pure . . . love of the ardent. Most of his drinking was conducted in single-handed contests, but occasionally he would invite [his colleagues], never more than one of them . . . at a time, and whenever he did his invariable parting injection was to 'mark twain,' meaning two chalk marks. . . . In this

way . . . he acquired the title which has since become famous
wherever . . . English . . . is read or spoken.[8]

Whatever the origins of his pen name, it clearly suited him;
he would employ it for the rest of his life, and it would
quickly evolve into a fully realized public persona that
would largely eclipse that of Sam Clemens.

It was also during his tenure on the *Enterprise* in December 1863 that Mark Twain would make friends with Southwestern humorist and platform lecturer Artemus Ward, who
was passing through Virginia City on a lecturing tour. Ward
tried without success to convince him that he was squandering his talent in the Nevada Territory, and that he should
accompany Ward back to New York to broaden his professional horizons. Twain would indeed soon be leaving the
territory—not for purposes of career advancement but
rather to avoid being thrown in jail.

Twain was gaining a reputation for his scathing satires of
the local officials and institutions of Virginia City, and in his
most recent, he had offended a prominent local women's organization. Though many readers were amused by the piece,
others were outraged. Twain soon found himself at odds with
the women in question, their husbands, and even a journalist
at another paper—the latter of which escalated into Twain's
issuing a pistoling duel. Though the duel never occurred, the
practice of dueling, or of even sending a challenge, was a
criminal offense in the territory, and Twain decided that it
would be prudent to leave the region while he was able. In the
wake of his departure, numerous territorial journalists
gloated in their columns over his having been run out of town,
but one journalist, John K. Lovejoy, editor of the *Daily Old
Piute*, lamented, "The world is blank—the universe worth but
57½, and we are childless. We shall miss Mark . . . to know him
was to love him. . . . We can't dwell on this subject; we can
only say—God bless you, Mark! Be virtuous and happy!"[9]

In May 1864 Twain was living in San Francisco, where he
would begin to write for the San Francisco *Morning Call*. It
was not long until he had also managed to offend local politicians and prominent businessmen in his column. After a
few months of employment, as Twain would later note, "[My
boss] invited me to resign my reportership on his paper, and
for some months I was without money or work."[10] Upon accepting his boss's "invitation," Twain made his way into the
Sierras to attempt gold prospecting yet again. Though he did

not find gold, he did discover treasure of another sort when he heard one of his fellow miners tell a particularly memorable folktale about a frog.

Twain soon straggled back into San Francisco, desperate and hungry. There he would learn, much to his surprise, that his distinctive journalism was gaining popularity on the East Coast (thanks in large part to Artemus Ward), and that he had begun to receive national acclaim as a Western humorist. This growing fame would generate enough freelance journalism for Twain to earn a living, and he soon wrote his own version of the frog folktale that he had recently heard, entitling it "The Celebrated Jumping Frog of Calaveras County." The story soon appeared in newspapers across the country, and it served to further his national exposure.

THE TRAVELING CORRESPONDENT

His budding fame as a Western humorist enabled Twain to negotiate a position with the Sacramento *Daily Union* as a traveling correspondent in the Sandwich Islands (known today as the Hawaiian Islands). He departed for the islands by ship in March 1866 and would spend four months in the islands, with the agreement that he would send back at least twenty letters. His stories were tremendously popular back in the United States, appearing in papers throughout the country. He rendered his fledgling literary persona in these letters as a well-mannered "straight man," and he invented a traveling companion named "Brown" to voice his more humorous and vulgar observations.

Upon his return to San Francisco, Twain was convinced by a local theater owner that he should capitalize on the popularity of his Sandwich Islands letters by giving a lecture about the islands. To the delight of his audience, he gave the lecture in the simplistic character and exaggerated Western dialect of his literary persona. The lecture was a rousing financial success as well, earning him the equivalent of several months' worth of journalism wages in one night. Based on this success, he embarked on a lecturing tour of the western United States, amassing an amount that, for him, was a small fortune. (Twain would return to lecturing again and again throughout his life for supplemental income.)

The success of Twain's Sandwich Islands letters compelled another newspaper, the *Alta California*, to hire him as its traveling correspondent to Europe and the Middle East.

In June 1867, Twain boarded the *Quaker City* bound for Europe. It was on this journey across the Atlantic—a crossing that he would make many more times in his life—that he first saw a miniature ivory carving, belonging to one of his shipmates, of the woman he would marry three years later. Biographer James M. Cox writes, "From the moment when, as Mark Twain remembered it, he saw the ivory miniature of her in her brother's stateroom in the *Quaker City*, she was, he confidently asserted, never out of his mind."[11]

Upon his return to the United States, Twain accompanied the former shipmate to his family home in Elmira, New York, to meet the woman whose carved image had so possessed him. Worldly, hard-drinking, chain-smoking, profane, and skeptical, Twain was the polar opposite of the frail, pious Olivia "Livy" Langdon, and he was something of an oddity in the home of her wealthy and sophisticated family. By the end of his three-week stay at the Langdon's, he had proposed to Olivia and had been firmly refused.

LITERARY BEGINNINGS

Twain's experiences while in Europe and the Holy Land were the basis of his first major book, *The Innocents Abroad*, published in 1869. Written during the promising post–Civil War era, amid booming industrialization and urban development, this travel book articulated America's emerging nationalism. As Twain scholar Dixon Wecter notes,

> Comic material was supplied by Clemens' fellow American tourists, who faced down . . . provincialism by brag and by cockalorum, and haggling over prices. Mark Twain gladly joined them, joking his way among the shrines and taboos of antiquity, comparing [Lake] Como unfavorably with Tahoe, bathing in the Jordan, finding any foreign tongue incredibly funny, and pitying ignorance, superstition, and lack of modern conveniences.[12]

The publication of *The Innocents Abroad* inaugurated a period during which it seemed that nothing could go wrong for Twain. Olivia had relented after a year of Twain's tireless courting, and the couple was married in February 1870. They moved into a large house in Buffalo, New York, which had been given to them by Livy's parents, and began to lead a life of marital bliss and affluence. On November 7, 1870, Olivia bore a son named Langdon Clemens. Two years later, Twain would publish his second book, *Roughing It*, which gave a humorous account of his experiences prospecting for gold in the Nevada Territory, and shortly thereafter, Olivia would give birth to their second child, Olivia Susan "Susy".

In June 1872 the initial euphoria of their life together came to a sudden halt when Langdon died of diphtheria. His death caused Livy such deep grief that Twain would decide to sell their new home in an effort to help her leave the tragedy behind. Within a year and a half, life had begun to brighten again. Livy's outlook had improved substantially, largely as a result of her new pregnancy, and a literary collaboration between Twain and Charles Dudley Warner—another native Missourian who had relocated to Hartford, Connecticut—yielded a commercially successful satirical novel entitled *The Gilded Age*. Twain's star was on the rise, and in June of 1874, Livy gave birth to daughter Clara Clemens.

Twain's recounting of his prospecting experiences in *Roughing It* had shown him that his past contained a wealth of creative inspiration. "The central drama of Clemens' mature literary life," suggests Twain scholar Justin Kaplan,

> was his discovery of a usable past—chiefly his boyhood in Hannibal, where his imagination continued to dwell for the rest of his days. . . . He began to make this discovery in his early and middle thirties—a classic watershed age for self-redefinition—as he explored the literary and psychological options of a newly created comic identity soon known the world over as Mark Twain.[15]

In 1875, Twain completed the manuscript of *The Adventures of Tom Sawyer*, in which he would recall the carefree aspects of his boyhood in Hannibal. Though Twain had initially intended the novel for adults, his friend William Dean Howells convinced him that it was primarily a story for boys. Following Howells's advice, Twain removed a few of the more irreverent passages and unsavory phrases before the novel was published in June 1876. Although initially marketed to boys, the novel enjoyed tremendous commercial success among children and adults alike. "The world of Tom Sawyer is gratifying to readers both adults and children," explains Everett Emerson. "In it wishes—even impossible ones—are granted, and the gratification is greater than in legends and fairy stories because the events in the book are not greatly removed from daily life."[14]

Pioneering an American Literature

Being largely self-educated, Twain was never instilled with the Victorian esthetic sensibility that most other American

In his later years, Twain spent much time in his private study.

writers had been taught to revere without question, and his unabashed anti-intellectualism had made his first literary efforts unique among the popular literature of the day. Though he knew well what good fun it had been to mock the European esthetic while writing *The Innocents Abroad*, the extent of his disdain for American writers who espoused that sensibility had been unknown to even himself until one particular evening in December of 1877.

Twain's publication in the *Atlantic*, a lofty New England literary journal, had been due in large part to his friend

Howells, who was now an editor for the magazine, and Twain's work had contrasted sharply with the more conventional works that had appeared with his. Along with revered American writers Ralph Waldo Emerson, Henry Longfellow, and Oliver Wendell Holmes, Twain had been invited to speak at a dinner in honor of fellow *Atlantic* contributor John Whittier. When it was Twain's turn at the podium, he told a story (in exaggerated Western accent and vernacular) of how three men had tricked a backwoods miner in California into thinking they were Emerson, Longfellow, and Holmes, and of how, upon learning from Twain that the men had been impostors, the miner had suspected that Twain was also merely an impostor posing as a writer.

Though Twain was himself blissfully oblivious to it, his satirical subtext was evidently clear to the majority of the audience: Emerson, Longfellow, and Holmes were literary phonies. Reportedly, with the exception of one unknown individual who was in hysterics, the audience was silently mortified by Twain's implication. Twain felt great remorse for the faux pax, and he later wrote letters to the three writers to beg their forgiveness. Notwithstanding his remorse, "Mark Twain and Howells knew that some buried force in the humorist had broken from control."[15] That "buried force," as critic Henry Nash Smith notes, continued to surface, as evidenced by Twain's even more overt contrasting of American sensibilities with those of Europeans in his next novel, *A Tramp Abroad*, published in March 1880.

December 1882 marked the publication of Twain's *The Prince and the Pauper*, which gives early evidence of Twain's desire to grow beyond the humorist confines that he had already imposed upon himself. Twain had written the work with the intent to publish it anonymously, for, as he noted at the time of its publication, "such grave and stately work [is] considered by the world to be above my proper level."[16] As with several of his future works, including *A Connecticut Yankee in King Arthur's Court* and *Joan of Arc*, this novel is set in medieval Europe, and calls attention to the injustices of tyranny. Though the novel would receive gratifying critical acclaim, it was a commercial disappointment.

RETURNING TO THE RIVER

Early in 1882 Twain took a six-week trip to Hannibal to recall his boyhood and to visit those of his childhood friends who remained there. With seventeen years having passed since his last visit, he was struck by the enormity of change that had taken place in Hannibal and on the river since his boyhood. The visit inspired him to begin work on two books simultaneously—one of them fiction, and the other non-fiction—and his working notes for the two books frequently overlapped. Common to the finished texts of both books is a passage that recalls the trademark boastfulness of the steamboat pilots that once resounded on the river:

> Whoo-oop! I'm the old original iron-jawed, brass-mounted copper-bellied corpse-maker from the wilds of Arkansas!— Look at me! I'm the man they call Sudden Death and General Desolation! Sired by a hurricane, dam'd by an earthquake, half-brother to the cholera, nearly related to the small-pox on the mother's side! Look at me! I take nineteen alligators and a bar'l of whiskey for breakfast when I'm in robust health, and a bushel of rattlesnakes and a dead body when I'm ailing! I split the everlasting rocks with my glance, and I squelch the thunder when I speak! Whoo-ooop! Stand back and give me room according to my strength! Blood's my natural drink, and the wails of the dying is music to my ear! Cast your eye on me, gentlemen!—and lay low and hold your breath, for I'm about to turn myself loose![17]

He finished the non-fiction book first, and it was published in May 1882. Entitled *Life on the Mississippi*, it employs vivid imagery and highly poetic language to provide a study of the great river and of the process of change in American life. The book was written largely from outside the humorous "Mark Twain" persona, however, and, as with *The Prince and the Pauper*, though it was deemed "legitimate" literature by critics, the novel had disappointing sales. As Dixon Wecter notes of *Life on the Mississippi*, notwithstanding its poor sales, Twain "long regarded it his greatest book—pleased with assurance to that effect from the German Kaiser and also from a hotel porter, whose praise he accepted with equal satisfaction."[18]

Twain found the second of the two river books, *The Adventures of Huckleberry Finn*, more troublesome than the first, and he would not complete it until 1885. "I never had such a fight over a book in my life before,"[19] he told Howells while writing it. Though the book is a sequel to the lighthearted *Tom Sawyer*, it incorporates the darker aspects of Twain's boyhood in Hannibal—most notably the institution of slavery. Huck's character is thus imbued with more complexity and adversity than Tom's; he is a homeless, ragged child of the river who, though suspicious of any attempt to "civilize" him, is grappling with the moral implications of slavery.

Not surprisingly, whereas Tom Sawyer's character had raised eyebrows among some parents and educators for his idleness and for having gotten the upper hand on adults through lying and disobedience, Huckleberry Finn's character was reacted to more strongly. Huck's decision to go to hell rather than to betray his friend, a runaway slave, for example, was considered unacceptable to the book banners of the day, and soon after its publication it was ejected from several public libraries, most notably that of Concord, Massachusetts.

MARK TWAIN'S FINANCIAL DISASTER

With *Huckleberry Finn*'s publication in 1885, Twain's fiction had reached a level of immense potency and complexity; however, his poor business judgment seemed also to have reached its peak, and he had invested an exorbitant amount of time and money into doomed financial schemes. He had financed his own publishing house, allowing his sister's son-in-law to run it, and had also invested heavily in the development of an automatic typesetting machine. He quietly backed the machine for five years, utterly convinced that it would one day make him a financial tycoon. By 1891, however, the typesetting machine had proved itself a complete failure. Though the machine had come close to anticipating the fabulous success of Merenthaler's Linotype, which would soon revolutionize the printing industry, its commercial failure cost Twain hundreds of thousands of dollars. Shortly thereafter, his publishing company went bankrupt as well.

Making matters worse was the fact that a man by the name of Will M. Clemens (no relation to Twain) had capitalized on their shared last name by writing *Mark Twain: The Story of His Life and Work* and publishing the book under his deceptively named "Clemens Publishing Company" in 1893. To maintain his carefully crafted public image, Twain had always denied the requests of biographers wishing to write his life story. His legal efforts to prevent this opportunist from publishing an unofficial biography had proved unsuccessful, however, and the seemingly official biography would enjoy significant commercial success.

The following year Twain completed *Pudd'nhead Wilson.* The acerbity of the observations made throughout the novel by its main character, Pudd'nhead, give evidence of Twain's own evolving views on the nature of the human race as well as his underlying desire to leave behind the constraints of lighthearted humor, which characterized his famous literary and public persona. "If you pick up a starving dog and make him prosperous," maintains Pudd'nhead, "he will not bite you. This is the principal difference between a dog and a man."[20]

By 1895 Twain's debts had grown astronomically, and he teetered on the brink of bankruptcy. Though he had come to flinch from his old role as platform zany, he saw no other choice than to embark on a round-the-world lecturing tour to recover his finances. Declaring bankruptcy was not an option for Mark Twain because it would have been harmful to his public image; he would instead become an exile overseas until such time as he could return to America to pay off his debts in full. Shortly after concluding his lecturing tour the following year, while resting in England, he received word that his eldest daughter Susy had died at Hartford of spinal meningitis. "It is one of the mysteries of our nature," Twain would later reflect on having received this news, "that a man, all unprepared can receive a thunder-stroke like that and live."[21]

Twain completed *Following the Equator* while living in England, and it was published in 1897. The book, which chronicled his recent round-the-world lecturing tour, employed the same brand of sure-fire burlesques of sentimental poetry, parodies of romantic situations, and flippancy at the expense of the peoples and customs of other countries that had made his other two travel books commercial successes. The American humorist's old recipe worked yet again, and the book was an overwhelming commercial success.

A HERO'S WELCOME

By 1900 Twain's fortunes and pride were sufficiently mended for him to return to America. He received a hero's welcome upon his return, and for the remainder of his life he would be the most conspicuous and widely admired American of his time, being as celebrated for his flamboyant white suits and his great mane of white hair as for his literary accomplishments. "The old rivertown urchin strutted among the gods of his time," notes biographer Ron Powers of Twain's life after repatriation. "His friendships had already touched the giants of the nineteenth century. . . . Now they expanded to embrace the coming Titans of the twentieth."[22] Among his new friends were future British prime minister Winston Churchill, Presidents Theodore Roosevelt and Woodrow Wilson, American business tycoon Andrew Carnegie, Russian revolutionary Maxim Gorky, and author Helen Keller.

Though in public he seemed to relish in his role as a living American legend, Twain came to feel increasingly alienated from society. He had seen during his travels abroad the cruelty of the human race and the bitter fruits of imperialism and industrialization. "Beneath his calculated outer wrappings," suggests Powers,

> [Twain] was a Mysterious Stranger, alienated and dream-driven, and the glint in his eye was not public amusement but private fury. A great dark river raged out of control through the vast channels of his being, a river that roiled against the foundations of his past, his friendships, his art; against mankind, against fate, against the Christian God, and against the fat and grasping nation that even now rushed out dumbly to worship him.[25]

Contributing to his despair had been the fact that, upon their return to America, Livy's health had begun to fail. After a prolonged illness, she died in 1904 of what her physicians diagnosed as organic heart disease and nervous prostration. With the exception of his two surviving daughters, Twain's entire family had already died by the time of Livy's passing, and after Livy's death, both of his daughters became estranged from him. The remainder of his days were spent without the comfort of the family that he had known all his life.

MARK TWAIN'S LAST YEARS

In 1906, at the age of seventy, Twain permitted noted biographer Albert Bigelow Paine to begin dictation on his official biography, with the understanding that it was to be published posthumously. A seamless blending of fact and fantasy, the biography was written entirely on Twain's terms, and Twain once came very near to firing Paine upon finding that he had sought information elsewhere regarding Twain's courtship of Livy. Twain had permitted Paine to write the biography not only to postpone the emergence of meddling, nonofficial biographies after his death but also to "restore integrity and direction to a rich, sprawling, and as he saw it, meaningless and pointless life."[24] The book took several years to complete and was then shelved by Paine.

In 1907 Twain completed *Captain Stormfield's Visit to Heaven*, a story that he had begun in 1868 but had discontinued because of Livy's opposition to its satirization of the Christian image of heaven. "Because of the circumstances of composition," notes Everett Emerson, "the story cannot be readily placed in Clemens's literary career."[25] The story is, nonetheless, widely considered to be one of his finest works, and it hearkens back to the time when Twain still took great joy in humor and satire.

The extent to which Mark Twain had endeared himself to the world by the beginning of the new century is evident in the honorary degree of doctor of literature that Oxford University conferred on him in 1907. Though he had received other honorary degrees, "The climax of his public career, he felt, was the honorary doctorate of letters which Oxford awarded him in 1907. . . . [Though there were also other famous honorees], the undergraduates at the ceremony, like the rest of England, reserved their loudest cheers for the American humorist."[26] Though Twain had always been proud of his having been self-educated, such certification of genius was irresistibly gratifying for a man who had been forced to leave school at the age of twelve.

Tragedy struck one last time in Twain's life on Christmas Eve 1909, when his daughter Jean suffered an epileptic seizure and drowned in her bath. Perhaps not wishing to also endure the death of Clara, his only remaining daughter and blood relative, Twain himself succumbed to heart disease a few months later at the age of seventy-four years and five months. "Before he slipped into coma," notes Justin Kaplan, "his last continuous talking was about 'the laws of mentality,' about Jekyll and Hyde and dual personality. To the end he remained as much an enigma and prodigy to himself as he was to the thousands at the Brick Presbyterian Church in New York who filed past the casket, topped with a single wreath of laurel, where he lay in a white suit."[27] Amazingly, Twain's prediction had been accurate—his death did indeed coincide with the reappearance of Halley's comet.

Twain's autobiography held sway over his posthumous image until 1920, when *The Ordeal of Mark Twain* by Van Wyck Brooks first sought to unmask the complex man behind the persona and to evaluate the impact of his real-life childhood on his literature and personality. Rebuttals to Brooks's conclusions quickly followed, thereby initiating a scholarly dialogue about Twain that endures to the present day and has yielded hundreds of books and thousands of journal articles encompassing the myriad aspects of his life and career.

This volume of Greenhaven's People Who Made History is intended to serve as an introduction to Mark Twain's enormous impact on American literature and society. It features some of the most recent and significant contributions to the vast body of Twain scholarship, including critical analyses of those formative experiences that culminated in young Sam's attainment of the stellar destiny of which his mother had assured him. Indepth viewpoints on the "Mark Twain" persona include investigations of its origins in his psyche, his decades of effort to cultivate and promote it, as well as the function that it ultimately serves in his literary works. His eclectic career as humorist, satirist, American booster, professional traveler, and platform lecturer is explored, as is the profound influence that he has had on his generation and those that have followed.

Nearly a century after his death, Twain's writings remain central to the American literary canon, their themes transcending historical eras and assuming new relevance for each new generation. Likewise, his popular appeal as the sage of the American experience is perhaps as vital today as it was during his own lifetime. Indeed, as with Halley's comet, it seems that Mark Twain's brilliance will continue to awe new generations ad infinitum.

NOTES

1. Quoted in Margaret Sanborn, *Mark Twain: The Bachelor Years.* New York: Doubleday, 1990, p. 3.
2. Sanborn, *Mark Twain*, p. 44.
3. Samuel Clemens, *Mark Twain's Autobiography.* New York: Harper & Brothers, 1924, p. 125.
4. Sanborn, *Mark Twain*, p. 104.
5. Justin Kaplan, ed., *Mark Twain: A Profile.* New York: Hill and Wang, 1967, p. xiii.
6. Ron Powers, *Dangerous Water: A Biography of the Boy Who Became Mark Twain.* New York: Basic Books, 1999, p. 285.
7. Everett Emerson, *The Authentic Mark Twain: A Literary Biography of Samuel L. Clemens.* Philadelphia: University of Pennsylvania Press, 1984, p. 10.
8. Quoted in Kaplan, *Mark Twain*, p. 163.
9. Quoted in Sanborn, *Mark Twain*, p. 241.
10. Clemens, *Mark Twain's Autobiography*, p. 242.

11. Quoted in Kaplan, *Mark Twain*, p. 193.

12. Quoted in Kaplan, *Mark Twain*, p. 7.

13. Kaplan, *Mark Twain*, p. vii.

14. Emerson, *The Authentic Mark Twain*, p. 82.

15. Quoted in Kaplan, *Mark Twain*, p. 176.

16. Quoted in Justin Kaplan, *Mr. Clemens and Mark Twain: A Biography.* New York: Simon & Schuster, 1966, p. 206.

17. Mark Twain, *Life on the Mississippi.* New York: Penguin Books, 1984, p. 15.

18. Quoted in Kaplan, *Mark Twain*, p. 23.

19. Quoted in Kaplan, *Mr. Clemens and Mark Twain*, pp. 248–249.

20. Quoted in Kaplan, *Mark Twain*, p. 26.

21. Quoted in Kaplan, *Mr. Clemens and Mark Twain*, p. 335.

22. Powers, *Dangerous Water*, p. 12.

23. Powers, *Dangerous Water*, pp. 8–9.

24. Kaplan, *Mark Twain*, p. xi.

25. Emerson, *The Authentic Mark Twain*, p. 112.

26. Hamlin Hill, *Mark Twain: God's Fool.* New York: Harper & Row, 1973, p. 175.

27. Kaplan, *Mr. Clemens and Mark Twain*, p. 338.

CHAPTER 1

Career-Shaping Experiences

PEOPLE
WHO MADE
HISTORY

MARK TWAIN

Mark Twain's Childhood

John Lauber

Having been born two months premature, Samuel Clemens (a.k.a. Mark Twain) was frail and sickly during early childhood, and the high mortality rate of children on the Mississippi Valley frontier left his parents uncertain as to whether he would survive. "Little Sam" beat the odds, however, and grew to be an unruly, mischievous boy with a wild imagination, and his childhood years in the colorful river-port town of Hannibal, Missouri, as well as on the nearby farm of his uncle John Quarles, would provide him with a rich source of creative inspiration throughout his lifetime.

In the following article, John Lauber analyzes some of Mark Twain's formative childhood experiences and influences, and compares Twain's real-life childhood with the embellished depictions given in his latter recollections and literary works. John Lauber was a specialist in American literature, he held a doctorate from the University of Washington and taught at the University of Alberta in Canada. He is the author of *The Inventions of Mark Twain* and *The Making of Mark Twain: A Biography.*

The frail boy grew stronger, and by the time he was nine, as his friend and official biographer, Albert Bigelow Paine, wrote, "the Tom Sawyer days may be said to have begun." On the Quarles farm and in Hannibal, young Sam was living the childhood that inspired *Tom Sawyer* and *Huckleberry Finn,* the early chapters of his *Autobiography,* as well as speeches and sketches and passages in other books till the end of his career. At first there seems no need to retell the story of Sam Clemens's childhood—Mark Twain has told it so well. But his

Excerpted from *The Making of Mark Twain,* by John Lauber (New York: American Heritage Press, 1985). Copyright © 1985 John Lauber. Reprinted by permission of the Estate of John Lauber.

matchless evocations of time and place, of a kind of childhood that can never be lived again, must not be taken as
records of fact. They leave out much: the father is absent,
Tom Sawyer is an orphan raised by his aunt. And much of
what they narrate did not happen. Mark Twain would always
be autobiographical, but he wrote autobiographical fiction
and fictional autobiography. "When I was younger I could remember everything, whether it happened or not," he once remarked, "but now I am getting old, and soon I shall remember only the latter." But long before he reached old age, he
could remember, intensely, the things that had not happened.

Of course, there can be no doubt that much of *Tom
Sawyer* is taken from life: probably young Sam gave
painkiller to the family cat, swindled his friends into white-
washing the fence, clobbered his younger brother for tat-
tling, escaped a whipping by calling out to his mother to look
behind her. He and his friends, like Tom and his gang, "used
to undress and play Robin Hood in . . . [their] shirt-tails, with
lath swords," in the nearby woods. He was mischievous and
troublesome enough, he had a reputation as "the worst boy,"
and twenty-five years later a Hannibal acquaintance in-
quired "if you still climb out on the roof of the house and
jump from third-story windows." The ritualistic fights with
other boys must have happened, too, although if Sam won
them as often as Tom did, it would have been through sheer
fury, not by size and strength. The picturesque superstitions
and folklore of *Tom Sawyer* and *Huckleberry Finn*—those too
are authentic. Sometimes they are grotesque—*"Barley-corn,
barley-corn, injun-meal shorts,/Spunk-water, spunk-water,
swaller these warts!"*—more often ominous, threatening
death by the howling of a dog, the cry of a whippoorwill, the
ticking of a deathwatch beetle. They can bring the terror of
ghosts, which "come sliding around in a shroud," says Huck,
"when you ain't noticing, and peep over your shoulder all of
a sudden and grit their teeth."

THE ORIGINS OF *TOM SAWYER* AND *HUCKLEBERRY FINN*

The geography of Hannibal and the surrounding region, of
the town itself, of the river and its islands, of Holliday's Hill
to the north and Lover's Leap to the south, of the nearby
cave, became the geography of Tom Sawyer's St. Petersburg.
But Tom's most dramatic adventures are imagined: Sam
Clemens never witnessed his own funeral, never saw a man

killed in a graveyard at midnight or testified at a trial for murder, never found hidden treasure, never was lost for days in a cave. *All* of the episodes showing the town's admiring attention focused on Tom are invented. *Tom Sawyer* is autobiographical fiction, drawn from memory of course, but memory shaped by imagination and desire.

It is misleading, then, to say, as his biographer, Paine, did and as Mark Twain himself did, that "[Twain's mother] Jane Clemens was the original of Tom Sawyer's Aunt Polly and the portrait is considered perfect." (For one thing, Sam's mother was just thirty-two at his birth, active and able, very different from Tom's elderly and ineffectual aunt.) Nor is it true that Nigger Jim "was" [the Quarles' slave] Uncle Dan'l, or that Huck Finn "was" a Hannibal playmate named Tom Blankenship—surely Huck "is" at least equally a reflection of the adult Mark Twain. Such claims seemed to lend authenticity, and Mark Twain liked to think of himself as a realist, but in practice he well understood that "by the privileges of our order we [writers] are independent of facts," and he used the privilege freely. Acknowledging that in *Huckleberry Finn* he had transformed the Quarles farm into the Phelps farm and moved it six hundred miles downriver, he adds that he "would move a state if the exigencies of literature required it." Like most books, also, *Tom Sawyer* derives in part from other books—the graveyard scene from [Charles] Dickens's *Tale of Two Cities,* the hunt for buried treasure from [Edgar Allan] Poe's "Gold Bug." And the relationship of Huck and Tom, with Huck playing literal-minded Sancho Panza to Tom's Don Quixote, must have been drawn from later reading of [Miguel de] Cervantes, not from boyhood reality. Tom's courtship of Becky Thatcher seems to have originated in Twain's unpublished fragment written in 1870, concerning "Billy Rogers" and "Amy," which may, in turn, have been meant to parody [Dickens's character] David Copperfield's courtship of Dora Spenlow, or even Mark Twain's own impassioned, just-completed wooing of his bride, Olivia Langdon.

As for Aunt Polly, supposedly copied from life, her characterization seems to owe as much to Mark Twain's recollections of Mrs. Partington, a popular character in newspaper humor of the 1850s, as to the reality of Jane Clemens. Like Aunt Polly, Mrs. Partington raises a mischievous nephew, Ike, but is too softhearted to do her duty by him and punish him as he deserves. Both Ike and Tom are mischievous but not malicious; both successfully "work" their aunts, steal doughnuts, play tricks on cats, misbehave in church, feign sickness to avoid school, and find inspiration in such books as *Black Avenger,* or *The Pirates of the Spanish Main.* So close was the resemblance between the two women that Twain's economical publisher actually used an illustration of Mrs. Partington to represent Aunt Polly in *Tom Sawyer.* One of Mark Twain's favorite stories about his own mother, that in her tenderheartedness she would warm the water in which she was going to drown the kittens, was also borrowed from the Partington pieces.

LIFE IN HANNIBAL

Of all Hannibal's gifts, the river was best—"the great Mississippi, the majestic, the magnificent Mississippi, rolling its mile-wide tide along, shining in the sun; the dense forest away on the other side; the 'point' above the town, and the 'point' below, bounding the river-glimpse and turning it into a sort of sea," as Mark Twain would describe it thirty years later in *Old Times on the Mississippi.* There was picnicking, swimming, skating, boating, with the boat "borrowed" more often than not—Sam and his gang once stole a skiff for the whole summer, painting it red for disguise. After several near-drownings, Sam Clemens finally became the best swimmer in his gang. In the summer, boys could escape to the Eden of Glasscock's Island, washed away a few years later by the irresistible river, to camp and swim and dig for turtle eggs and go naked in the sun. . . .

There was the excitement of steamboat arrivals, bringing the sleepy little town to life with the cry "S-t-e-a-mboat a-comin'!"—the boat gorgeous with gilt and glass and gingerbread, flag flying bravely and tall twin chimneys belching thick, black smoke, a dramatic effect created by throwing carefully hoarded pitch pine on the fires as the town came into view around the bend. The steamboat was central to the lives of Sam and his friends; we may remember Ben Rogers, in *Tom Sawyer,* "impersonating the Big Missouri and . . . drawing nine feet of water," and simultaneously taking the parts of boat, captain, and engine bells. It was the dream of every boy to go on the river, to taste the glamor and excitement of its life. And a surprising number of them, including Sam Clemens, were to realize that dream.

But a boy's life could not be lived entirely in freedom, on the river or the farm. School and church, the institutions of culture, loomed forbiddingly; somehow the reluctant Sam had to conform to their requirements as best he could, since it was unthinkable that they should conform to him. On his first day at school, aged five, he broke a rule and was switched; the pattern of his schooling had been set. His older sister, Pamela, had won a certificate for "amiable deportment and faithful application," but Sam took no prize for either quality. To a restless and imaginative boy, school brought torturing boredom; it was a place where children "devoted . . . eight or ten hours a day to learning incomprehensible rubbish by heart out of books and reciting it by rote, like parrots," where they memorized and delivered hackneyed "declamatory gems" such as [Lord] Byron's *"The Assyrian came down like a wolf on the fold,/And his cohorts were gleaming in purple and gold."* He excelled only in the weekly spelling bees, which offered the thrill of competition.

Discipline was arbitrary, often brutal—although as remembered in *Tom Sawyer*, the worst beatings never seemed to hurt. The second school that Sam attended was kept by a Mr. Cross. That wonderfully appropriate name inspired the boy's first known writing:

Cross by name and cross by nature—
Cross jumped over an Irish potato.

School taught him reading, writing, and arithmetic, and a smattering of history and geography; it exposed him to literature, generally moralistic; it sought to inculcate the virtues of industry, patriotism, and piety; it tried to make him a Model Boy—and failed utterly. His real education would come later.

THE INFLUENCE OF RELIGION

The Sabbath too brought boredom and fear, fear of damnation and hell rather than of the master's stick—a deeper, more spiritual, and longer-lasting terror. Sunday commenced with family worship, led by Jane Clemens, beginning "with a prayer built from the ground up of solid courses of scriptural quotations . . . and from the summit of this she delivered a grim chapter of the Mosaic Law." Then came Sunday school, teaching Sam that bad boys went to Hell and were likely to die early. Finally the Presbyterian sermon had to be endured:

The minister droned along monotonously through an argument that was so prosy that many a head by and by began to nod—and yet it was an argument that dealt in limitless fire and brimstone and thinned the predestined elect down to a company so small as to be hardly worth saving.

That sermon was heard by Tom Sawyer, but Sam Clemens must have suffered through its counterparts. The Presbyterianism of the Mississippi Valley seems to have been a rigorous Calvinism, a religion of "free grace and preforeordestination," as Huck Finn puts it—demanding perfection while insisting on the total depravity of the human race, giving to God the power and the right, in His inscrutable wisdom, to save those whom He chose to save and damn those whom He chose to damn.

Religion permeated the culture of pioneer Missouri. There might have been dissenting freethinkers—[Sam's father] John Clemens might have been one—but they kept their heresy to themselves. Besides the weekly ritual of family worship, Sunday school, and sermon, with an evening service occasionally added as punishment for any extraordinary crime that Sam might have committed, there was the frenzy of the camp meetings, which were to reappear in *Huckleberry Finn,* and of the periodic revivals in town. Not to share in their enthusiasm was to be an outcast from Hannibal as well as from Heaven. When Tom Sawyer recovered from an illness and learned that during his sickness all his friends had been "saved," "he crept home to bed realizing that he alone of all the town was lost, forever and forever," and that the raging storm outside was aimed at his sinful self: "He covered his head with the bedclothes and waited in a horror of suspense for his doom." The eye of God was upon him and punishment would surely come, in this world and in the next. Sam Clemens must have endured such terrifying experiences; before his childhood ended, he had learned to know the Bible, to fear God—the wrathful, implacable, all-seeing Calvinist God—and to feel guilt. That guilt might be unreasonable, exaggerated, completely without cause—but no matter. To be human was to be guilty.

CLASS DIVISIONS AND SLAVERY

There were lessons to be learned from the town as well, realities of class and race. Outwardly, as Mark Twain remembered, Hannibal might have seemed "a little democracy . . .

full of Liberty, Equality and Fourth of July," but for all the civic piety and readings of the Declaration of Independence, it was a Southern town, and the "aristocratic taint was there." Class distinctions were clearly drawn, and the Clemenses, with more pride than property, suffering the periodic humiliations of forced moves and sheriff's sales, must have felt them painfully. At the top of the scale were the well-to-do professional men, wearing their tall hats and swallow-tailed coats, and owning land and slaves. By right of birth and education, John Clemens felt that he belonged to that class, but he could never earn the income needed to live as they lived. Below these "gentry," Hannibal had its respectable middle class, its workingmen, and its outcast poor whites, like Jimmy Finn, the town drunkard, or the disreputable Blankenships. Young Tom Blankenship, as Mark Twain remembered him, was "ignorant, unwashed, insufficiently fed," but goodhearted and independent, "the only really independent person . . . in the community—therefore happy and envied by other boys." Naturally his society was forbidden to boys of respectable families, and naturally "the prohibition doubled and quadrupled its value."

Beneath all whites were the blacks. Slavery was unquestioned; "the wise, and the good and the holy," Mark Twain recalled in his *Autobiography*, unanimously held that the institution was righteous and sacred, "the peculiar pet of the deity, and a condition which the slave himself ought to be daily and nightly thankful for." No one, at least to young Sam's knowledge, "seemed conscious that slavery was a bald, grotesque, and unwarrantable assumption." Doubters would have kept silent in any case; in the rural Missouri of the 1840s or 50s, to criticize slavery would have been to invite lynching. Denying the existence of God would have been safer. John Clemens apparently had no qualms about the institution; in 1841 he served on a jury that sentenced three abolitionists to prison terms of twelve years each for inciting slaves to escape. Mark Twain would observe, from his own experience, that it was a mistake to say that slavery made Southern whites hardhearted in general; it "merely stupefied everybody's humanity as regarded the slave." He had evidence for that in his own boyhood home. The Clemenses owned one slave—a girl named Jennie—during Sam's early childhood, and he remembered once seeing his father beat her with a bridle for insolence; Judge Clemens cuffed, too, the small black boy whom they hired from his master "for any little blunder or awkwardness," and occasionally gave him a lashing "which terrified the poor thing nearly out of his wits." Yet John Clemens was otherwise a humane man.

There were no great plantations nearby, and slavery as Sam knew it was of the "mild domestic variety." Yet the reality could not be avoided. Like every Southern town, Hannibal had its despised "nigger-trader"—he made a convenient scapegoat—and once Sam saw "a dozen black men and women, chained together waiting shipment to a Southern slave market." Harsh brutality was frowned on by decent whites but could not be prevented. Mark Twain would not forget "the slave man who was struck down with a chunk of slag for some small offense; I saw him die." Once the corpse of a slave, drowned while trying to escape and then "much mutilated" by his white pursuers, rose out of the river mud to terrify Sam and his friends. Although a reward was offered, one of the Blankenships had kept the man's hiding place secret all summer and occasionally brought him food— behavior that Twain must have recalled when he had Huck decide to help Nigger Jim escape.

The two races were in intimate, daily contact, and white and black children could, almost, be comrades. Mark Twain would remember that he "was playmate to all the niggers, preferring their society to that of the elect." But "complete fusion" could not occur; "color and condition imposed a subtle line"—subtle, yet a barrier that not even children could ever shut out of consciousness. Sam Clemens accepted slavery, as boys do accept the basic institutions of their society; he grew up with all the unquestioned prejudices of the Southern white and even served briefly in a Confederate militia unit at the outbreak of the Civil War.

Then, having left the South forever, he became aware, over the years, of his attitudes and worked to change them, doing his part to pay the debt that he came to feel every white man owed to every black man. He helped to finance the studies of a black artist in Paris and to pay the way of a black student through Yale Law School; he urged President Garfield to retain the black leader Frederick Douglass as marshal of the District of Columbia; he read and lectured in black churches; in his old age he composed "The United States of Lyncherdom," a searing indictment of the moral cowardice by which the decent majority permitted lynching. In "Which Was the

Dream," a late fragment, he even created a black avenger, the mulatto Jasper, who inverts the relation of master and slave, mercilessly blackmailing a white man and forcing him to undergo every cruelty and degradation that Jasper has suffered from the white race in a lifetime. Mark Twain became, said his friend William Dean Howells, "the most desouthernized Southerner" that Howells had ever known. Yet childhood conditioning could not be completely overcome; he once confessed to Howells that he had hired George Griffin, the black butler at his Hartford mansion, because he could not bear giving orders to a white man, and in his dreams a dark-skinned woman would signify sexual abandon.

The Harshness of Life on the Frontier

Life in Hannibal was uncertain, precarious; as the townspeople must have been reminded every Sunday, death could come at any moment, in the home or on the street. The sick died at home, without drugs, often conscious to the end, and no family could escape the deathbed ritual, with a ring of mourners around the sufferer, waiting to make their good-bys and to hear the final words. The Clemenses knew that experience three times during Sam's childhood: with the death of nine-year-old Margaret from "bilious fever," just before the move to Hannibal; of Benjamin, age ten, in 1842—Sam would never forget how his mother had knelt beside the bed, holding his hand and moaning "while the tears were flowing down her cheeks unchecked"; and with his father's death five years later.

Violence was frequent, too, in that apparently peaceful town. Young Sam saw things there he could never blot from his memory. One evening, while John Clemens was serving as justice of the peace, Sam entered his father's empty office and saw in the moonlight the corpse of a murdered man stretched out on the floor, brought there to await an inquest. As an adult, he told the story humorously: "I went out at the window, and I carried the sash along with me; I did not need the sash, but it was handier to take it than it was to leave it, and so I took it." But it could not have been a joke then.

Murder could be committed on the streets and go unpunished. The shooting of Boggs by Colonel Sherburn, one of the most famous scenes in *Huckleberry Finn*, probably had its origin in the killing of Sam Smarr, a noisy but harmless drunk, by William Owsley, a prosperous merchant whom

Smarr had insulted. Owsley shot down the defenseless man "in the mainstreet at noonday" and walked away unmolested. Sam Clemens saw "the grotesque final scenes—the great family Bible spread open on the profane old man's chest." In his nightmares he himself "gasped and struggled for breath under the crush of that vast book for many a year." That detail was to appear in *Huckleberry Finn*. A year later the murderer was tried and acquitted. Hannibal was a Southern town, it acknowledged a gentleman's right to protect his honor—and Owsley would have had his friends, who might have taken revenge on a jury that voted to convict.

LIFE IN HANNIBAL

Mark Twain would return time and time again in his literature to his river-front hometown of Hannibal, Missouri. In the following passage from Life on the Mississippi, *published in 1883, he vividly recalls the sights, sounds, and smells of Hannibal.*

Once a day a cheap, gaudy packet arrived upward from St. Louis, and another downward from Keokuk. Before these events, the day was glorious with expectancy; after them, the day was a dead and empty thing. Not only the boys, but the whole village, felt this. After all these years I can picture that old time to myself now, just as it was then: the white town drowsing in the sunshine of a summer's morning; the streets empty, or pretty nearly so; one or two clerks sitting in front of the Water Street stores, with their splint-bottomed chairs, tilted back against the walls, chins on breasts, hats slouched over their faces, asleep—with shingle-shavings enough around to show what broke them down; a sow and a litter of pigs loafing along the sidewalk, doing a good business in watermelon rinds and seeds; two or three lonely little freight piles scattered about the "levee"; a pile of "skids" on the slope of the stone-paved wharf, and the fragrant town drunkard asleep in the shadow of them; two or three wood flats at the head of the wharf, but nobody to listen to the peaceful lapping of the wavelets against them; the great Mississippi, the majestic, the magnificent Mississippi, rolling its mile-wide tide along, shining in the sun; the dense forest away on the other side; the "point" above the town, and the "point" below, bounding the river-glimpse and turning it into a sort of sea, and withal a very still and brilliant and lonely one.

Mark Twain, *Life on the Mississippi*, 1994.

Violence, like slavery, was a part of Mark Twain's heritage and, again like slavery, would finally taint all his recollections of the South.

THE THREAT OF POVERTY

Things went badly for the Clemenses in Hannibal. Creditors pressed them hard, they moved frequently, there was a sheriff's sale in 1843 and another ordered in December 1846—but the sheriff found nothing left to seize. There might be recoveries, times when John Clemens could afford to buy a piano for his daughter or speculate, unsuccessfully, in silkworm culture or even build a new house, a cramped little dwelling with low ceilings and a ladderlike stairway on a lot twenty and a half feet wide, now preserved as Mark Twain's boyhood home. But the trend was downward. John Clemens kept store again, and again the store failed; land and buildings were lost; the slave girl was sold; [Sam's brother] Orion was apprenticed to a printer in St. Louis—much against his will, for he felt that he was a gentleman's son and deserved a profession, while printing was only a mechanical trade. Then Orion realized that he was following in the footsteps of Benjamin Franklin. Franklin records in his autobiography that as a young man he lived for a time on a diet of biscuits and water, and Orion decided to imitate his famous model. His mind "cleared amazingly," he felt, but biscuits and water did not make a Franklin.

The father's schemes seemed only to lead to more expense. In the winter of 1841–42 he made a long journey into the South, hoping to collect a debt. He took with him a new slave, Charley, apparently bought as a speculation, expecting to sell him for "whatever he will bring." Charley brought ten barrels of tar, the only return from the trip. The debtor was in difficulties, and John Clemens was too softhearted to press for payment, although he had traveled hundreds of miles through winter rain and snow to collect that debt. Reading his father's letters many years later, Mark Twain was struck by the contrast between his humanity toward the white man and the casual indifference of his reference to the slave, "as if he had been an ox—and somebody else's ox." The journey had been a costly failure. Orion would remember hearing his mother reproach her husband for the useless expense, and his father answering, "with a hopeless expression," that he "was not able to dig in the streets."

He tried to practice law, but cases were few; he worked as a clerk in another man's counting house; he served as justice of the peace "and lived on its meager pickings," as Mark Twain would recall. Meager they certainly were; in the Owsley case, Justice Clemens earned $13.50 for writing documents totaling 13,500 words, and $1.81 for swearing in twenty-nine witnesses. Each move marked a decline; the family had no fixed home. Once Orion returned from St. Louis without warning, late at night, went to the last address, where, according to family tradition, he silently climbed the stairs to his old room, undressed in the dark, and found himself in bed with two strange women—sisters of the new occupant. Final disaster came in 1846, when even the furniture was lost and the Clemenses were reduced to sharing quarters with another family for whom Mrs. Clemens cooked. . . .

Life in poverty, or under its perpetual threat, left Sam with a lifelong horror of debt. But it did more than that: it made him constantly aware of the need for money, of the humiliating discrepancy between family pretensions and family realities; forced him to prove his success and status by extravagant spending, to yearn to be really rich, even when he was already a wealthy man, and to indulge in obsessive, ruinous speculating. He required absolute security, and there could never be enough money to guarantee that.

Mark Twain's Lecturing Apprenticeship

Fred W. Lorch

Mark Twain earned fame and fortune for over four decades as a platform lecturer by exhibiting what appeared to be a natural gift for public address. In the following essay, Fred W. Lorch argues that the seemingly effortless deadpan humor and potent storytelling skills that would come to characterize Twain's lectures were in fact the result of many years of apprenticeship under master storytellers, beginning with his own relatives and their slaves, and ending with famous Southwestern humorist and platform lecturer Artemus Ward. The late Fred W. Lorch was head of the Department of English and Speech of Iowa State University between 1942 and 1949, and his articles on Mark Twain have appeared in many of the leading scholarly journals in the field of American literature.

The fact is that, during his early years, the most effective preparation for Mark Twain's career as a public speaker came in ways so subtle and undetected that at the time neither he nor his family and friends ever suspected them of possessing any influence at all. This preparation came primarily through his exposure to a number of exceptionally able raconteurs and his own gradual absorption of their skills. The importance of this has long been recognized in the development of Mark Twain as a writer, but has not been sufficiently emphasized in his development as a public lecturer and reader. . . .

Nor did [Twain biographer] Albert Bigelow Paine sufficiently perceive its importance to Mark Twain's platform career. His assertion that most of Mark Twain's attainments came as a natural gift has dubious validity. It certainly does

Excerpted from *The Trouble Begins at Eight*, by Fred W. Lorch (Ames: Iowa State University Press). Copyright © 1968 The Iowa State University Press. Reprinted by permission of the publisher.

not account adequately for Mark Twain's skill as a story-teller. The truth is that few American platform celebrities preceding Mark Twain experienced a more extensive and impressive apprenticeship in the art of storytelling than he.

Fortunately, his association with masterful raconteurs came at a very early age. Most influential of all, probably, was his mother. As a child and as a growing boy he was not consciously aware of the moving power of her speech, but years later he remembered it and paid it a warm tribute. "There was something moving in her voice and manner," he recalled,

> that was irresistibly pathetic. . . . I know now that she was the most eloquent person whom I have met in all my days, but I did not know it then. . . . I had been abroad in the world for twenty years and known and listened to many of the best talk-ers before it at last dawned upon me that in the matter of moving and pathetic eloquence none of them was the equal of that untrained and artless talker . . . that obscure little woman with . . . the great heart and the enchanted tongue.

STORYTELLERS ON THE FRONTIER

But in those early years Mark Twain had the high fortune of listening to other masterful raconteurs besides his mother. One of the earliest and most impressive was his father's slave, Uncle Ned. It was from him that Mark Twain heard, and never forgot, the ghost story, The Golden Arm, with its star-tling climax which later became one of his most successful readings on the public platform. It was during these early years, also, that he heard and never forgot the stories told at his Uncle John Quarles' farm, near Florida, Missouri, where, up to the age of twelve, he spent most of his summers.

According to local tradition, John Quarles possessed a ready and hilarious wit, was brilliant in repartee, and a born storyteller. Sam Clemens greatly admired his mirth-loving uncle, who contrasted so pleasantly with his silent and stern-faced father, and listened to his stories with rapt atten-tion. It was probably from John Quarles that Mark Twain first heard the Jumping Frog story, an ancestral version of the one he later heard in the barroom at Angel's Camp in California. But no less influential were the old spirituals and stories of mystery, magic, and imagination which he en-countered in the slave quarters—stories by Aunt Hanner and Uncle Dan'l, the latter known to readers of *The Adventures of Huckleberry Finn* as Jim—both wonderful storytellers. Some of these yarns were so vivid and delightful, or hair-raising, that they stayed in his memory throughout his life and served him often and well both in his books and on the platform. There can be little doubt that during these early and formative years Mark Twain's imagination was shaped not so much by books as by talkers—by storytellers whose untutored and seemingly simple art brought life and magic to their recitals and stamped them forever upon his memory.

By the time the farm days were over and the death of his father in 1847 made it necessary for him to go to work, his love and respect for accomplished storytellers were deeply rooted. Thereafter, whenever he met good raconteurs, he listened to their yarns with absorbed interest. In Ament's print shop in Hannibal, for instance, where Sam was an apprentice for a time, there was Pet McMurray, a journeyman printer in his twenties who was full of stories. Typical of journeymen at the time, he was a carefree drifter who had been many places and seen many things. If he failed to find work in his own profession, he turned to lecturing on temperance. All McMurray wanted, Mark Twain later recalled, was a plate, a bed, and enough money to get drunk on. In some respects he resembled the Duke in *The Adventures of Huckleberry Finn*, though there is nothing to indicate that he was quite so disreputable a character. In Ament's shop, also, was Wales McCormick, a large lad of eighteen whose hilarious sense of humor, practical jokes, and stories amused and sometimes irritated Sam. But both McMurray and McCormick were excellent storytellers, and Mark Twain never forgot them.

In the years that followed, Mark Twain's wanderings and his various employments brought him in contact with an ever widening circle of raconteurs. There were the endless stories he heard in the pilot houses of Mississippi steamboats, in the ships' bars, and in the Pilots' Association rooms in St. Louis, Memphis, Baton Rouge, and New Orleans. And after the war had closed the river and he had gone west with Orion [his brother, who had been appointed Nevada Territorial Secretary by President Lincoln], he encountered a whole new world of storytellers—in the mining camps, in the saloons, and in the newspaper offices of Virginia City, Carson City, and San Francisco.

One of the richest bonanzas Mark Twain struck in oral literature occurred in the winter of 1864–65, when a series of circumstances took him down to the Twolumne district of

California to spend an indefinite period with his old friend Jim Gillis, a pocket miner and gambler who lived in a cabin on Jackass Hill. Sharing the cabin with Gillis were his younger brother William, Dick Stoker (Dick Baker in *Roughing It*), and Dick's cat, Tom Quartz. When bad weather stopped mining activities, the long days and nights were often spent in storytelling. Years later he remembered those scenes, especially the rainy days when they all gathered about the fireplace and listened to Jim, with his back to the warmth, tell stories of his own creation, "forged as he went along." For the most part, as Mark Twain recalled, Gillis' stories usually consisted of the wonderful adventures of his companion Dick Stoker, "portrayed with humor and that serene and vagrant fancy which builds as it goes, careless as to whither it is proceeding and whether the story shall end well or ill, soon or late, if ever."

It was from Jim Gillis, that winter in the Twolumne Hills, that he heard the delightful story of Dick Baker's cat (Tom Quartz), the Jay Bird and the Acorn, and the Burning Shame (which later found its way into *The Adventures of Huckleberry Finn*). That same winter in a saloon at Angel's Camp, he heard Ben Coon, a solemn and drowsy-witted old ex-Illinois river pilot, tell in a slow monotonous way the story of the Jumping Frog. What caught Mark Twain's fancy on this occasion was not so much the substance of the tale (he had probably heard other versions of it, as we have seen), but the exquisite absurdity of Coon's manner of telling the story without betraying a single hint that he regarded it as humorous.

THE BEGINNING OF TWAIN'S LECTURE CAREER

As a result of his long and impressive tutelage under master raconteurs it is inevitable that Mark Twain should himself have become a talker and a skilled storyteller. No better example of his ability as a raconteur, before he ever became famous on the platform, could be offered than an incident that occurred one evening in San Francisco, in 1864 or 1865, when he was working as a reporter for the *Morning Call*. A group of his associates had planned to attend the theater and had met in one of their rooms. Presently Mark Twain drifted in, sat down on the end of a bed, and began telling stories. They listened with such absorbed interest that the theater was entirely forgotten, and it was near midnight before the storytelling had ended.

Mark Twain

The most evident beginning in Mark Twain's career as a public speaker, however, took place in Carson City in the winter of 1863–64. Mark Twain had gone west in the summer of 1861, when the outbreak of war had closed the Mississippi. For a time he had worked with Orion, serving in an unofficial capacity as secretary to the Secretary. Then, after a brief, unsuccessful try at silver mining in various Nevada communities, he became a reporter on the Virginia City *Enterprise.* It was while working for this paper that he reported the sessions of the Nevada Territorial Legislature sitting at Carson City. His popularity among the legislators soon became so great that on the evening of December 11, 1863, immediately after the close of the Constitutional Convention held in Nevada that year, Mark Twain was elected President of the Third House, and given the honorary title of "Governor." A unique institution in the American scene, the Third House was a mock legislature organized for the purpose of burlesquing the issues, debates, and personalities of the regular legislative sessions. It elected its own slate of "state officials," and made fun of the legislative processes in general.

Mark Twain's delightfully dead-pan report of the procedures of the meeting on the night of December 11 appeared in the *Enterprise* a few days later. Concerning his remarks in acknowledgment of his election as "Governor" he reported himself merely as saying: "Gentlemen: This is the proudest moment of my life. I shall always think so. I shall ponder over it with unspeakable emotion down to the latest syllable of recorded time. It shall be my earnest endeavor to give entire satisfaction in the high and bully position to which you have elevated me."

Thereupon the real fun of the evening began with Mark Twain presiding as President of the House and revealing his awareness of the mannerisms of the various legislators who had risen to speak by burlesquing the "I . . . ah, I . . . ah" manner of Legislator Youngs and the annoying habit of buttoning and unbuttoning his coat by Mr. Ralston.

The Third House was to have its opening meeting toward the end of January, 1864, while the regular legislative session was still in progress. At that time "Governor" Mark Twain was scheduled to deliver the annual message. In the meantime, the Constitutional Convention having ended, he returned to Virginia City to resume his routine reporting of local news for the *Enterprise*. But the events that took place during the next few weeks were anything but routine. In fact, for his future career as a public lecturer they were momentous.

The excitement which presently developed in Virginia City was caused by the appearance of Artemus Ward, celebrated humorist, writer, and lecturer, who had speaking engagements in Virginia City, Carson City, and other towns in the district. Artemus Ward, then in his thirtieth year, was at the pinnacle of his career and tremendously popular. He had just arrived from San Francisco where he had lectured to enthusiastic houses. He had planned to stay only a few days in Virginia City, but he was so captivated by the genial companions he found there, particularly in the office of the *Enterprise*, that he could not bear to leave till the end of the month. . . .

ARTEMUS WARD'S INFLUENCE

Ward's influence upon Mark Twain as a lecturer . . . is . . . difficult to assess. Conclusions concerning it can be based only upon inference and supposition. Though it is highly probable that Ward may have narrated some of his lecturing experiences to Mark Twain, there are no indications that he offered advice about lecturing or that he even suspected his journalist friend of having ambitions for platform success. Had he stayed in Nevada long enough to hear Mark Twain deliver his "Governor's" message to the Third House, the story might have been different. At the moment, however, he was merely aware that the *Enterprise* reporter was a most engaging talker and a splendid storyteller.

Nor is there any evidence that Mark Twain consciously examined Ward's platform manners and techniques, at this time, for the purpose of employing them himself at some future occasion. As a reporter, however, whose duty it was to cover Ward's lecture Babes in the Wood for the *Enterprise*, it must be assumed that he listened to the great showman's performance with absorbed interest, and observed his platform art. It is probable, also, after the lecture, especially after Mark Twain's report of it appeared in the *Enterprise*, that the two men found an opportunity to discuss briefly, at least, the art of a humorous lecture and the most effective means of making an audience laugh.

Unfortunately, Mark Twain's review of Ward's lecture in Virginia City has not been preserved since the files of the *Enterprise* for the years when Mark Twain worked for the paper are no longer extant. . . .

Whether or not Mark Twain offered an extended analysis of Ward's platform manner and technique for the benefit of his readers cannot now be established. They could scarcely, however, have escaped his attention—the dead-pan facial expression even at the most humor-provoking passages, the casualness of his manner, the simulated unconsciousness that anything funny had been said, the feigned look of surprise when the audience laughed, the pause and the use of anticlimax by "dropping a studied remark, apparently without knowing it, as if one were thinking aloud." That he was deeply impressed by the performance is evident. Eight years later, during the season of 1871–72, he included Artemus Ward in his lecture Reminiscences of Some Uncommonplace Characters I Have Chanced to Meet. And when that lecture failed, he prepared a new one devoted entirely to Ward, as the most compelling and important uncommonplace character in his repertoire. In that lecture Mark Twain drew heavily upon his observations of the man he had admired so much during the Virginia City days.

The time came years later when Mark Twain's early admiration for Ward's platform technique diminished somewhat, as he realized that there had been too much technique about his lectures. There were too many tricks, too often repeated. Though delightfully humorous on first hearing, they did not stand repetition well. People learned the tricks. They could anticipate them, see them coming. One of the perfections of Mark Twain's mature artistry, on the other hand, was to prevent the artistry from "showing through." His humor, compared with Ward's, seemed natural, rather than contrived. In 1863, however, his admiration for Ward's artistry on the platform appears to have been unqualified, nor does he appear at this time to have questioned the propriety of Ward's use of the content of his lecture merely for the purpose of extracting humor [though Twain would eventually employ humor as a means to convey a deeper moral message].

Nevertheless, one must conclude that during his Virginia City visit, Artemus Ward did exert a powerful influence upon Mark Twain's later platform career. Never before had Mark Twain had the opportunity to observe a humorist perform with such consummate skill on the platform. If the devices and techniques which produced such floods of laughter were not new to him, the finesse with which they were employed, and the studied artistry behind the seeming casualness and simplicity of Ward's manner, were impressive. Beyond anything he had ever observed or imagined possible, Ward's lecture showed him how a master performer completely captured an audience with humor by a clever manipulation of techniques and an exploitation of manner. Whether or not the impact of observing Ward's artistry at the time set him dreaming of seeing himself on the platform, capturing audiences with humorous lectures in a similar way, cannot be determined. More important is the fact that he absorbed what he saw, and when the time came to face his own paying audiences a few years later, he consciously attempted to adapt them to his own platform personality, materials, and purposes.

TWAIN'S "GOVERNOR'S MESSAGE" SPEECH

Within a week or two after Ward's departure from Virginia City, Mark Twain was back in Carson City reporting the new session of the territorial legislature. Also he was now busy preparing his Governor's Message to the Third House, scheduled for January 27. As this date neared, the trustees of the Presbyterian Church in Carson City, to which Orion belonged, addressed a letter to Mark Twain, asking him to help them raise funds for their unfinished church building. They suggested an admission charge of one dollar each for the privilege of listening to his "communication."

The request appeared in the Carson City *Daily Independent* on January 23, 1864, and Mark Twain's reply [stating that he would grant their request] appeared in the same paper on the same day. . . .

According to Clement Rice, a reporter for Virginia City *Daily Union,* who had attended the lecture, "a large and fashionable audience" turned out to watch the fun and to hear Mark Twain orate, and when the evening was over, two hundred dollars had been collected toward the completion of the church. . . .

Mark Twain's report of his speech appeared in the *Enterprise* the next day. It throws further light on his performance and offers a bit of self-criticism.

> I delivered that Message last night, but I didn't talk loud enough—people in the far end of the hall could not hear me. They said "Louder—louder" occasionally, but I thought that was a way they had—a joke, as it were. I had never talked to a crowd before, and knew none of the tactics of the public speaker. I suppose I spoke loud enough for some houses, but not for that District Courtroom, which is about seventy-five feet from floor to roof, and has no ceiling. I hope the people will deal as mildly with me, as I did with the public officers in the Annual Message. Some folks heard the entire document, though—there is some comfort in that. Hon. Mr. Claggett, Speaker Simmons of the inferior House, Hon. Hal Clayton, Speaker of the Third House, Judge Haydon, Dr. Alban, and others whose opinions are entitled to weight, said they would travel several miles to hear that message again. It affords me a good deal of satisfaction to mention it. It serves to show that if the audience could have heard me distinctly, they would have appreciated the wisdom thus conferred upon them. They seemed to appreciate what they did hear though, pretty thoroughly. After the first quarter of an hour I ceased to whisper, and became audible. One of these days when I get time, I will correct, amend, and publish the message, in accordance with a resolution of the Third House ordering 300,000 copies in the various languages spoken at the present day.

> P.S. Sandy Baldwin and Theodore Winters heard that message, anyhow, and by thunder they appreciated it, too. They have sent a hundred dollars apiece to San Francisco this morning, to purchase a watch [and] chain for His Excellency Governor Twain. I guess that is a pretty good result for an incipient oratorical slouch like me, isn't it? I don't know that anybody tendered the other Governor a testimonial of any kind. . . .

To what extent Mark Twain, either consciously or unconsciously, employed the manners and techniques in the Governor's Message which characterized his later performances on the lecture platform is impossible to say. So far as is known, no one who was present in the Presbyterian Church that evening later described it in written form with sufficient particularity to make a firm judgment about the matter. It is highly probable, however, that in personality, manner, and technique he was entirely himself and that no one felt that he was well known in the Washoe area. Everyone knew that his slow drawling manner of speech was genuine. And if, during the Message, he employed such devices as dead-pan humor, an assumption of casualness, veiled shrewdness, and the pause, one may be sure that all of them were techniques he had long been familiar with and had long ago absorbed in his own art of storytelling. . . .

With the Governor's Message behind him, the major phases of Mark Twain's apprenticeship for a career on the public platform came to an end. His actual experience on the platform during the formative years had been brief though impressive. On the other hand his long exposure to expert raconteurs had been exceptionally rich and rewarding, and his love for talking and storytelling had spurred him on.

Piloting the Mississippi

Ron Powers

Ron Powers suggests that Samuel Clemens felt a deep, lifelong connection to the Mississippi River—so much so, in fact, the river was for him a symbol of life itself. Powers argues that Clemens's brief career as a riverboat pilot, during which he studied the river's every nuance, would permanently and profoundly alter his perceptions of the river, and consequently, his perceptions of life. Powers employs this "river-as-life" metaphor to illustrate how Clemens's piloting knowledge caused his simplistic assumptions about life—and perhaps life as a southerner in particular—to give way to an awareness of the powerful, often contradictory forces at work beneath the illusory surface of things. This paradoxical knowledge that he had gleaned from the river would continue to inform his writing and chameleon-like Mark Twain persona throughout his career. Powers also notes that the immense cross-section of humanity that comprised the riverboat culture of the Mississippi would provide Mark Twain with a rich pallet of characters and dialects to use in his fiction. Ron Powers is author of *Dangerous Waters: A Biography of the Boy Who Became Mark Twain* and *White Town Drowsing: Journeys to Hannibal.*

On April 15, 1857, Sam Clemens made the break from his landlocked life. More decisively, in the short run at least, than leaving [his hometown of] Hannibal, he left the world of safe employment, the world of dry ground, and hit the river for adventure. At age twenty-one, he booked passage on the steamboat *Paul Jones,* out of Cincinnati, bound westward on the Ohio and then down the Mississippi for New Orleans. His plan, manifestly, was to find a seagoing ship that would get him to South America. Unfortunately for his Amazon

Excerpted from *Dangerous Waters,* by Ron Powers. Copyright © 1999 by Ron Powers. Reprinted by permission of Basic Books, a member of Perseus Books, L.L.C.

dreams and Henry Clemens [his younger brother who died in a riverboat explosion while trying to follow in Sam's footsteps], and fortunately for American literature, the pilot of the *Paul Jones* had a sore foot and a malleable turn of mind. By the time the boat docked at New Orleans eleven days later, Sam had talked his way onto the [piloting] deck, had taken over most of the steering, and had become convinced that his real destiny was to steer riverboats for a living.

The pilot's name was Horace Bixby. A small sturdy man of thirty-one when Sam Clemens made his intrusion, he had a prominent nose, a firmly set mouth, and hair brushed all the way across his head from a low part. He would survive a steamboat explosion near New Madrid, Missouri in 1858, pilot heroically for the Union flotilla during the Civil War, achieve greatness in his trade, and outlive Mark Twain by two years, dying a few months after the *Titanic* sank in 1912, in a St. Louis suburb. Thus he lived to see the full effusion and even share the celebrityhood unleashed by his indulgence of the small, drawling young man suddenly at his elbow on the Ohio River, where the young man was now for the second time being conceived.

In Mark Twain's semifictionalized remembrance of his first encounter with Bixby, he retained the affect of a boy, rather than a twenty-one-year-old man. Once the "ancient tub" is under way down-river, for instance, he was overcome with a boy's exultant sense of being a king, "bound for mysterious lands and distant climes."

> . . . when we stopped at villages and wood-yards, I could not help lolling carelessly upon the railings of the boiler-deck to enjoy the envy of the country boys on the bank. If they did not seem to discover me, I presently sneezed to attract their attention, or moved to a position where they could not help seeing me. And as soon as I knew they saw me I gaped and stretched, and gave other signs of being mightily bored with travelling.

THE LANGUAGE OF THE RIVER

A good deal more revealing than that set-piece bit of cuteness, perhaps, is his revelation a few paragraphs later of his delight in the *language* that washed over him on board—the rich, profane vernacular of the rivermen:

> "Here, now, start that gang-plank for'ard! Lively, now! *What*'re you about! Snatch it! *Snatch* it! There! There! Aft again! aft again! Don't you hear me? Dash it to dash! Are you going to *sleep* over it! Vast heaving. '*Vast* heaving, I tell you!

Going to heave it clear astern? WHERE're you
barrel! *For'ard* with it 'fore I make you swal'
dash-dash-*dashed* split between a tired r
crippled hearse-horse!"

I wished I could talk like that.

He could, of course, and did; ultimately such a passage
mimetic Twain, talking. The passage, and many others like
it in *Life on the Mississippi,* suggest that Sam Clemens's at-
traction to the river derived as much from the human language peculiar to the river culture as from the river itself.
(Indisputably, he heard money talking as well: river-pilots'
"princely" salaries, up to $250 a month, were legendary in
the country then, and Sam would forever be drawn to the
prospect of the big payday.) River and language, in any case,
would soon be conjoined in his creative consciousness. His
language would flow like a river; his books, never tightly
plotted, would seem instead to follow some mysterious
course of their own making—shifting channels, eroding certain boundaries, flooding at times, running nearly dry at
others, spilling over capriciously onto the high ground. As
for the river itself, he learned to "read" it, and the river became a wonderful book, "a book that was a dead language to
the uneducated . . . but which told its mind to me without re-
serve, delivering its most cherished secrets as clearly as if it
had uttered them with a voice."

Twain even seems to drop a prophetic reprimand, a para-
graph later, to the literary clinicians of the century to come.
An overemphasis of the river as text, he warns, has hazards
of its own to give:

> Now when I had mastered the language of this water and had
> come to know every trifling feature that bordered the great
> river as familiarly as I knew the letters of the alphabet, I had
> made a valuable acquisition. But I had lost something, too. I
> had lost something which could never be restored to me
> while I lived. All the grace, the beauty, the poetry had gone
> out of the majestic river!

But all that mastery, and all that loss, were yet to come.
His first agenda aboard the *Paul Jones* was to somehow meet
the pilot and get control of the wheel.

Horace Bixby himself recalled to the biographer Paine
that his first awareness of Sam Clemens was as a voice—a
"slow, pleasant voice" that spoke up one sunlit day from behind his shoulder as he steered the boat along toward St.
Louis. The voice wanted to know whether Bixby would like

each a young man the river. Bixby thought he wouldn't ke it at all. But the voice itself caught his attention. "What makes you pull your words that way?" he remembered asking; and the answer came back, more slowly still and in some way irresistibly comic, "You'll have to ask my mother. She pulls hers, too."

Then the owner of the voice—"a rather slender, loose-limbed young fellow with a fair, girlish complexion and a great tangle of auburn hair"—took a seat on the visitors bench a few feet from the wheel and asked Bixby whether he knew the Bowen brothers. Bixby said he did; he'd supervised Will Bowen's first steering. "A mighty good boy, too. Had a Testament in his pocket when he came aboard; in a week's time he had it swapped for a deck of cards." The auburn-haired youth replied that Will, Sam, and Bart had been schoolmates of his in Hannibal. Bixby asked him whether he drank, gambled, swore, or chewed. The young man replied that he did not. Well, qualify that: in terms of swearing, "Not for amusement; only under pressure." It occurred to Bixby that he could use a little relief for his sore foot. He sat down and let the young man take the wheel. "Keep her as she is—toward that lower cottonwood snag." The Amazon receded; the Mississippi swelled.

It was in New Orleans that Sam launched his plea to Bixby for a position as an apprentice, or cub pilot. Before he did that, he apparently made some last inquiries around town about whether it would be possible to make a boat connection to the Amazon. (It wasn't.) He and Bixby agreed on terms: $500, of which $100 must be paid in advance. (In *Life on the Mississippi,* Mark Twain suggests that the bargaining occurred during a "three-day seige" en route downriver from Cincinnati.) The *Paul Jones* left New Orleans for St. Louis on April 30, where Sam set about rounding up the money. He called on his wealthy distant cousin James Clemens again, and again left without satisfaction: "Before I got to the subject he was wailing about having to pay $25,000 taxes in N.Y. City—said it makes a man poor! So I didn't ask him." Sam was luckier with William A. Moffett, [his sister] Pamela's husband. He secured a loan, presented it as the deposit, closed the agreement with Bixby, and on May 22, he and his mentor were steaming back down to New Orleans aboard the *Crescent City,* his career as a riverboat pilot contractually underway.

LEARNING THE RIVER

The river distance between St. Louis and New Orleans—Bixby's essential territory—was thirteen hundred miles. Every mile bore its distinct feature: river width, river depth, location of the channel, the presence of underwater snags, rocks, shoals, and previously sunken watercraft, including giant steamers. Sam's first revelation regarding the immensity of his chosen trade was that he would have to memorize the river. Mile by mile. His second revelation was that his education had begun before he knew it—Bixby's habit of mentioning landmarks to him on that first downriver passage had not been a matter of idle chitchat. Mark Twain made great semifictional sport of this—[Twain biographer] James Cox has likened the episodes to a series of vaudeville acts—in his reminiscences:

> Presently he turned on me and said:—
>
> > "What's the name of the first point above New Orleans?"
>
> > I was gratified to be able to answer promptly, and I did.
>
> I said I didn't know.

But it wasn't a matter of sport at the time. Sam's third revelation was that he had to memorize the river in both directions: memorize twenty-six hundred miles of river, that is; or, more accurately, memorize two separate rivers, given not only that the visual prospect was utterly different, but also that a boat behaved quite differently with the flow behind it than it did breasting the current.

His fourth revelation was that he had to retain a mental image of the *shape* of the river, the river entire, for there were times when the river's particularized contours could not matter. As Bixby explained: "It is all there is left to steer by on a very dark night. Everything else is blotted out and gone." That was the easy part. "But mind you, it [hasn't] the same shape in the night that it has in the daytime."

The fifth and final revelation, following quickly on the fourth, was that the imprinted shape of the river entire did not matter ultimately anyway, given that the river entire never sustained itself, as [ancient Greek philosopher] Heraclitus saw, from one second to the next. The river's banks were constantly caving in, new channels constantly spilling across dry land, new islands constantly being formed and obliterated, and land that had been Missouri property one day reemerging as a part of Illinois the next.

These revelations may well have been fictionalized compressions of more subtle and complex processes by which Sam Clemens learned the pilot's trade. But to the extent that they are true—and their irreducible truth has not been contradicted by scholarship—they suggest an elemental conversion in Sam's lifelong comprehension of the river.

The river, it was turning out, was never exactly what it appeared to be. The river was a chimera, a memory.

The river that he had known since childhood—the greatest constant in his oft-disrupted life, more enduring even than his family—this river, the Father of Waters—did not, in certain ways of thinking of it, exist. Certainly it did not flow into or out of a world that could be understood in terms of the rational, the predictable, the sunlit. The river was a dream, dark and mystical, forever evanescent, yet forever in terrible control of the lives of mortal men. The dream was dangerous—dangerous water; that's what the leadsman's cry of "mark twain" essentially meant: two marks, two fathoms, twelve feet, the bottom rushing up from the depths to scrape and threaten and capsize the craft. The danger of running aground was his most searing association with the cry of *"Mark* twain":

Then came the leadsman's sepulchral cry:

"D-e-e-p four!"

Deep four in a bottomless crossing! The terror of it took my breath away.

"M-a-r-k three! . . . M-a-r-k three . . . Quarter less three! . . . Half twain!"

This was frightful! I seized the bell-ropes and stopped the engines.

"Quarter twain! Quarter twain! *Mark* twain!"

I was helpless. I did not know what in the world to do. I was quaking from head to foot, and I could have hung my hat on my eyes, they stuck out so far.

"Quarter *less* twain! Nine and a *half!*"

. . . My hands were in a nervous flutter. I could not ring a bell intelligibly with them. I flew to the speaking-tube and shouted to the engineer,—

"Oh, Ben, if you love me, *back* her! Quick, Ben! Oh, back the immortal *soul* out of her!"

The consummating irony here is that Sam's peril is itself an illusion, his terror a construct of Horace Bixby's mentoring strategies. The "crossing"[1] in this incident was not shallow at all, a fact that Sam had already committed to memory. Bixby had instructed the leadsman to call out false depths as a way of testing Sam's courage and his confidence in his own knowledge of the river.

What it may have done, in some incremental way (along with a thousand other episodes of unreliable perception), is reinforce an abiding metaphor in Mark Twain's life and work: that things are seldom what they seem, reality and illusion being deeply intertwined. The river was awash in dualities; it ceaselessly reinvented itself; it switched identities; it was its own twin, upstream and down. Its deceptively sweet currents masked deeply encoded messages. Its many interconnected stretches, running fast and slow, straight and curved, were dialects that needed close attention. Wreckage lay strewn below the surface. Danger was the only constant of life on the phantasmal Mississippi; that is to say, of life. . . .

THE CHARACTERS OF THE RIVER

[Mark Twain] reaped another substantial dividend from his river-years, one that he did not hesitate to describe in terms of capital gain:

> I am to this day profiting somewhat by that experience; for in that brief, sharp schooling, I got personally and familiarly acquainted with about all the different types of human nature that are to be found in fiction, biography, or history. . . . When I find a well-drawn character in fiction or biography, I generally take a warm personal interest in him, for the reason that I have known him before—known him on the river.

He found there, in other words, the mother lode of human character: character even more diverse and abject and vivid than he was to encounter in Nevada, the land of the mother lode itself. On the river he found characters who (as has been said of the characters in *The Great Gatsby,* who share subtle affinities) were constantly in the act of self-revelation. Illusion always existed in tension with the hard facts. River characters were blunt prolific talkers, for the most part, giving to Twain's ear the stripped-down, high-velocity pitch

---

1. A "crossing" was a lateral movement by a pilot seeking to maneuver his boat from one side of the river to the other in search of the deepest water. Crossings were frequent, and called forth the pilot's greatest navigational skills and most intimate knowledge of the river's varying depths.

that he hurled into the thick upholstery of American letters. River characters talked in jargon, in a thousand jargons: pilots, roustabouts, officers, hustlers, slaves, refined women, unrefined women, Europeans, mystics, soldiers, killers, the clergy. Collectively they offered up a constant bonanza of language and predicament.

Sam may or may not have written it all down—there is little evidence that he did—but he invested it somehow, and when the time came to draw interest, it was all there, waiting. The effect of those years, as [Twain biographer Bernard] DeVoto said, is visible in Mark Twain's perception of the human animal. He imported those effects off the river and into his books. *Tom Sawyer* may have been possible without the river years, but certainly not *Huckleberry Finn, Pudd'nhead Wilson, The Gilded Age, The American Claimant,* any number of his essays and sketches—to say nothing of the vast and enigmatic *Life on the Mississippi.* [American author] T.S. Eliot was right in calling him a servant of the river-god.

The Nevada Territory

James M. Cox

Samuel Clemens boarded a stagecoach bound for the Nevada Territory in July 1861 with the intention of assisting his brother Orion with his duties as territorial secretary. Shortly after his arrival, however, Clemens was instead traversing the harsh Nevada desert in search of the elusive Comstock Lode—an immense vein of silver and gold which lay beneath the stretch of land on which Virginia City would soon be built.

In the following essay, James M. Cox suggests that, whereas Samuel Clemens was born in Hannibal, Missouri, in 1835, Mark Twain was born twenty-eight years later in the Nevada Territory. Cox asserts that Clemens's failure as a prospector was central to his conceiving of the "Mark Twain" persona, and also suggests that it was during this era that Clemens began, albeit unconsciously, to change his position on slavery and the Civil War. James M. Cox is author of *Mark Twain: The Fate of Humor*.

For the biographer, the life of Mark Twain begins on November 30, 1835, in Florida, Missouri, with the birth of Samuel Clemens. But for the critic it begins on February 3, 1863, with Samuel Clemens' discovery of his pseudonym "Mark Twain" in the Nevada Territory. On that date, in the Virginia City *Territorial Enterprise,* the name was affixed to a humorous travel letter describing an "exciting" trip with a talkative companion named Joe Goodman, who in the course of four hours managed to utter three or four words. The Joe Goodman of the sketch was the impassive foil to the suffering traveler Mark Twain; he was the first of a long line of buffoons who were to encumber the pilgrimage of the deadpan Mark Twain, who would in turn become one of the world's great travelers.

The two figures in the sketch—a pair created for the purposes of comedy—had their counterparts in reality. Joseph

Goodman was the immensely capable editor of the *Enterprise;* Mark Twain was his star reporter. It is possible that Samuel Clemens had used the pseudonym in earlier letters—this "first" letter alludes to prior experiences, as if Mark Twain were no neophyte making his debut. But if Mark Twain had a recorded comic past, it is not likely ever to emerge, for the files of the *Enterprise* have been lost. The chief reason, and a good one, for believing the February 3 exercise to be the first appearance of Mark Twain is that Goodman, whose entire life reveals a rare integrity, remembered the event as having occurred on February 2, 1863, which is only one day off.

Mark Twain is hardly more than a name at first; he scarcely possesses a personality in any sense of the word. All that the first brief and somewhat crudely funny letter reveals is a minimal humorous perspective. Yet it was to the development and fulfillment of this perspective that the entire imaginative powers of Samuel Clemens were to address themselves. In the name Mark Twain, Clemens had discovered much more than a mere pseudonym. He had discovered his genius, his authentic signature; and his discovery, though he could not have known it at the time, became the event around which his life was to be reorganized.

Precisely because it was such an event, it is also the point at which to begin critical discussion of Mark Twain. With another writer the logical point might be the first book, but with Mark Twain it is the signature itself which constitutes the first distinct *work.* The moment such a decision is made, certain striking significances assert themselves and Mark Twain is disclosed in a new light which, though it may not illuminate all recesses, reveals a new writer against a new background. Instead of beginning with the culture of the Midwest frontier, or with the scars of childhood, we begin with a writer who is "born" at the age of twenty-eight. And instead of beginning with the society of Hannibal, Missouri, in the age of Jackson, we begin with the Nevada Territory at the height of the Civil War. Finally, instead of examining the genealogy of the Clemens family, we begin with the pseudonym "Mark Twain" and all the meanings it had and came to have. The aim of such a beginning is neither to evade the complex issues of Samuel Clemens' early life nor to ignore the frontier literary tradition he exploited, but to discover how Mark Twain reorganized his past and how he triumphed over the traditions he inherited.

THE POLITICAL AND ECONOMIC CLIMATE OF THE NEVADA TERRITORY

Mark Twain was "born" in the territory of Nevada, one month after the Emancipation Proclamation. "I feel," writes this territorial figure in the first sentence of his career, "very much as if I had just awakened out of a long sleep." Thus, almost as if he were Rip Van Winkle, Mark Twain makes his debut in American literature. And there is a sense in which Mark Twain is the true progeny of Rip. Rip had slept through the American Revolution, returning to the new America to find his whole identity in jeopardy; Mark Twain had slept through the Civil War—had slept through the inner division of his country—and he would ultimately return to a different America from the one Samuel Clemens had known on the west bank of the Mississippi River before the war.

It would be easy to say he slept because the war was remote from Virginia City, but the fact is that Nevada, from within as well as from without, was defined by the Civil War. From without, Abraham Lincoln was engaging in overt political maneuvers in an effort to accelerate Nevada's admission to the Union and thus add another pro-Union state legislature which would in turn make possible the ratification of the Thirteenth Amendment abolishing slavery. From within, the populace was split on the matter of the Civil War. Although Union sentiment prevailed, there was widespread Secession sympathy. The name of the chief metropolis, Virginia City, attested the territory's Southern past. Prominent Southerners such as William Gavin, Henry S. Foote, Colonel Davis S. Terry, and General William Walker had been struggling to swing neighboring California to the Southern side. Terry became governor of the newly created Nevada Territory in March, 1860. Though Lincoln's election diminished Secessionist power in Nevada, there were open demonstrations on the part of the "Secesh" after the [Confederate victory in the] battle of Bull Run; and though the battles of Virginia were remote from Virginia City, the issues of the Civil War cut directly across the entire territory, at once determining and defining territorial politics.

More important than the Civil War in Nevada was the discovery of silver. If the national issue of slavery gave Nevada political significance, silver gave it substance. Without the silver there would have been no population, no territory, no statehood, no community. Nevada would have remained no more than a vast and desolate extension of [head of the Mormon Church] Brigham Young's Utah Territory. But with the discovery of the Comstock Lode in 1859, settlers and investors poured into Washoe—as the territory was called—and by 1861, despite Young's attempt to thwart secession, what had been Carson County, Utah, became the Nevada Territory, and Virginia City became the second great city of the West.

The entire economic reality of Nevada lay in its mines. California had become great because of its gold, but it had many other assets—good land, timber, water power, and a magnificent coast—to sustain it after the gold rush abated. Nevada had nothing but desert. True, the Mormons had made agricultural settlements in the few river valleys in an effort to remain a political force capable of contending with the gold seekers flooding into Carson County, but they abruptly departed when Brigham Young recalled them to aid him against the assembling forces of the Federal Government. After their departure, only the mines and sporadic industries remained.

Twain Evades the Slavery Issue

This was the territory into which Samuel Clemens came in the summer of 1861. In a sense he was admirably suited to the nature of the place. If it was not fully committed to the Civil War, neither was he. He had been a lieutenant in the Confederate Army in the spring of 1861 and had retreated for two hectic weeks before "resigning"—as he drolly referred to his desertion. Later in the summer he came West with his brother Orion, a strong Union man who had been appointed Territorial Secretary for Nevada by Lincoln in return for active aid in the campaign of 1860. Though it is inaccurate to say that Samuel Clemens fled from the war, it is inadequate to insist that he was an innocent child who had no mind of his own, that he did not realize the seriousness of the slavery issue, and, having entered boyishly and thoughtlessly into the war, just as innocently deserted when he realized that the war led to killing his fellow men. This is the explanation Mark Twain was to give 24 years later in "The Private History of a Campaign that Failed." But Mark Twain's "private" history of Samuel Clemens' experience in the war is as much a burlesque of all the public histories then appearing in the *Century Magazine* as it is a confession of Samuel Clemens' behavior in the war.

Samuel Clemens' actual response to the Civil War will perhaps never be known, but it is absurd to think that a twenty-five-year-old able-bodied young man who had held the exacting and responsible position of steamboat pilot on the great Mississippi had no knowledge about the slavery issue. Nor is it enough to say that Samuel Clemens really did not want to be a Southerner but simply went along with the heavy pressures of society. After all, his brother Orion had freed himself to become an active abolitionist. Samuel Clemens' early letters home from New York and Philadelphia show that he was actively Southern in his sympathies. He deplores the rise of the black man in the North and on the whole sounds little like the desouthernized Southerner William Dean Howells was later to know. "I reckon I had better black my face," he wrote to his mother from New York, "for in these Eastern States niggers are considerably better than white people."

Clemens' reconstruction as a Union man took place in Nevada, but it was no sudden conversion. Henry Nash Smith has convincingly shown that the realignment did not begin to be complete until late 1862. As late as February 28, 1862—six months after arriving in Nevada—Clemens was still referring to Union forces as "they." On March 8, he sarcastically observed to his friend William Claggett of a gentleman named Sewall, "He is a Yankee,—and I naturally love a Yankee." Not until September 9, 1862, did his pronoun designating Union forces become "we," and even when he identified himself with the North, he scathingly criticized Union braggadoccio. It was during this period of realignment from Southerner to Union man that "Mark Twain" was discovered. Yet through all the territorial discord generated by war issues Mark Twain remained essentially silent. This silence would be relatively inconsequential if slavery and the Civil War past played no major part in the world Mark Twain was to reconstruct; but slavery becomes one of his major—perhaps *the* major—concern in *Huckleberry Finn, A Connecticut Yankee,* and *Pudd'nhead Wilson.*

The confrontation of slavery lay far ahead. At the time Mark Twain was discovered, Samuel Clemens was essentially evading the issues of the Civil War. In that early and confusing time, the pseudonym may have provided, among other things, a means of evasion and escape, just as, much later, it would constitute a means of confrontation. Certainly the territory, though it might feel the issues of the war, was an excellent realm in which to sidestep the public pressure of the war. The territory, though a legal organization under protection of the Federal Government, did not pay taxes to the Government. [Historian and poet] Carl Sandburg observes that the reason Nebraska did not join the Union earlier was that the territorial legislature did not wish to pay taxes. Admission cost too much. Beyond all this, the territory was an uncommitted region which had the geographical shape of a state without the character and responsibilities of statehood. The territories had been the safety valves which released mounting pressure for Civil War. They were, historically speaking, the means by which the entire nation was able to delay the growing conflict between North and South. As the territories diminished with the admission of new states, the unresolved differences between North and South became more and more acute, and the means of compromise became less and less available.

THE SEARCH FOR RICHES

If Samuel Clemens avoided the slavery issue, he by no means avoided the silver fields. He might have to wait until much later to discover how he actually had felt about slavery and the Civil War, but his speculative sense of adventure, excitement, and a world of possibility came quickly and vigorously to the surface. Not surprisingly, his first distinctive humorous quality emerges out of a commitment to the extravagant and grandiose dream of territorial glory. It is evident in the first letter he wrote to his mother from Nevada. Refusing to invite her until she can be received in "style," he sets out to detail the quality of the area, first by an inclusive list of Nevada's riches—a list which begins with gold and ends with jackass rabbits. After describing the desolation by faintly burlesquing Biblical language, he expands into this fantasy:

> I said we are situated in a flat, sandy desert. True. And surrounded on all sides by such prodigious mountains that when you stand at a distance from Carson and gaze at them awhile,—until, by mentally measuring them, and comparing them with things of smaller size, you begin to conceive of their grandeur, and next to feel their vastness expanding your soul like a balloon, and ultimately find yourself growing, and

swelling, and spreading into a colossus,—I say when this point is reached, you look disdainfully down upon the insignificant village of Carson, reposing like a cheap print away yonder at the foot of the big hills, and in that instant you are seized with a burning desire to stretch forth your hand, put the city in your pocket, and walk off with it.

Although there is nothing particularly original in the substance of the fantasy, there is an impulse to dramatize, to *play*. The fantasy takes its departure not in the form of a vernacular character's actions—as in the case of Davy Crockett—but from the literary mind's activity under the pressure of a particular kind of space. The result is the invention of a Brobdingnagian figure who at once expresses and burlesques the romantic attitude of identification with nature. The comic impulse of the letter exploits the inadequacy of the clichés of travel literature to describe the desolation of a new landscape. But the humor, the emotional quality of the letter, emerges from the point of view. The person writing the letter is not angry or disillusioned by the discrepancy; he discharges both anger and disillusion by exaggerating the discrepancy, thereby converting it into an imaginative playground—a field for invention.

The subsequent letters to his mother during the winter and spring of 1861–62 show beyond a doubt that Samuel Clemens' quest for gold and his discovery of himself were one and the same thing. These letters chronicle his travels over the great vacant stretches of Nevada in search of gold and silver. They are not private letters describing suffering and doubt, but public travel letters—many of them were published in the Keokuk *Gate City* almost as soon as they were received—transforming the futility of the journey into the humor of excessive suffering. In two of them, the writer, referring to himself as the bard, begins by burlesquing poetry. Inventing his reader—in this case his mother—in the role of an innocent Aunt Polly relying on literary and travelbook tradition, he good-naturedly undertakes to tease her out of her clichés and ignorance in the process of educating her. In order to dramatize his correspondent, he has to dramatize himself as the prodigal son who will one day entertain his mother in the grand style. His generosity is predicated upon the boundless hope of discovering wealth; the gold is always the illusion which sustains his generous and audacious idea of himself.

FAILURE LEADS TO SUCCESS

His humor arises from his awareness that he is the fool of his illusion, but the awareness is no direct communication of disillusion or despair; instead it is a conversion of the futility of the quest into a comic odyssey in which landscape, inhabitants, and the journey itself become the absurd resistances to the illusion. In such a humorous vision, the mere device of investing an animal with elaborate human psychology becomes a genuinely imaginative event. Clemens' description of the horse Bunker and the dog Curney reveal a rapidly maturing writer. Of Bunker, who had accompanied the prospecting party on the Nevada expedition, he wrote:

> But it was on Bunker's account, principally, that we pushed behind the wagon. For whenever we came to a hard piece of road, that poor, lean, infatuated cuss would fall into a deep reverie about something or other, and stop perfectly still, and it would generally take a vast amount of black-snaking and shoving and profanity to get him started again; and as soon as he was fairly under way, he would take up the thread of his reflections where he left off, and go on thinking, and pondering, and getting himself more and more mixed up and tangled in his subject, until he would get regularly stuck again, and stop to review the question.

By transferring to the horse what would otherwise be, and no doubt were, the narrator's feelings and thoughts of futility, Samuel Clemens was investing the world with an absurd humanity it had hitherto lacked.

His humor arises from the act of exploiting the discrepancy between futile illusion—not merely his own, but those of society and history—and "reality." The humorist's creative role lay in inventing a "reality" which would define the inadequacy of the given traditions, clichés, and illusions. Thus in these early letters to his mother he already shows a mastery of this technique of invention. Asserting that she has asked him to tell her about the "lordly sons of the forest sweeping over the plains on their fiery steeds," he devotes an entire letter *not* to demolishing the illusion of the Indian but to the creation of a grotesque Indian who will seem more "real" than the cliché. Asking her to imagine an Indian called Hoop-de-doodle-doo, he first outlines his ignoble red man's appearance—slouched and slovenly in the cast-off clothes he has been given by whites. . . . Clemens' Indian is no more real or realistic than [*Last of the Mohicans* author James Fenimore] Cooper's. The truth of the vision depends not upon its accuracy but upon its commitment to exaggeration and contrast. In that commitment, which so exceeds the reader's expectations, lies the authority of Samuel Clemens' imagination and the distinction of his humor. Cooper is not being attacked so much as he is being belittled by the exaggerative play of the humorous imagination.

In the same way that he used Cooper, Clemens used his whole futile quest for gold. His discovery of himself as a writer depended upon the failure, not the success, of his quest. He had to fail as a prospector and later as a speculator so that he could succeed as a writer, for his very invention of himself as a writer is based not upon finding the proverbial pot of gold but upon discovering *nothing*—nothing but the resources of the comic imagination which can elaborate the futility of the territory into the material of humor. Thus, after utterly failing to find gold or silver in the Nevada Territory, Samuel Clemens became a reporter on the Virginia City *Territorial Enterprise*. From that seemingly unpromising claim in the literary world, he went on to discover Mark Twain and fortune.

CHAPTER 2

The Mark Twain Persona

The Function of Persona in Mark Twain's Literature

Don Florence

Though it is tempting for readers to try to unveil the "real" man behind Mark Twain's literary works, Don Florence suggests that they need to accept Twain's literary persona on its own terms if they wish to appreciate its true genius. Florence notes, however, that even while accepting Twain's literary persona at face value, readers may still find themselves doubting his credibility as a narrator, as it often seems as if his perception of his predicament in his early "autobiographical" tales is grossly distorted. Florence concedes that Twain's narrative perspective is indeed subjective, and he suggests that it is precisely this narrative subjectivity, this dubious accounting of his situation, which constitutes the triumph of his literary persona. Whereas in real life there is pain and confusion over the reconciling of one's inherently subjective perspective with an ever-changing, often-incomprehensible outside world, Mark Twain's literary persona refuses to be hostage to such disparities. He instead embraces and glorifies the inherent subjectivity of the human psyche by employing ironic humor as a means of interpreting reality, of undercutting this seeming reality of life and circumstance, and ultimately, of transcending his narrative plight. Don Florence is author of *Persona and Humor in Mark Twain's Early Writings*.

In general, Twain's early writings are presented as "narrative histories" that direct us to the implied author behind them. Interweaving fact and fiction, these narratives are fictive truths, or better yet, true fictions. They are presented as

Reprinted from *Persona and Humor in Mark Twain's Early Writings*, by Don Florence, by permission of the University of Missouri Press. Copyright © 1995 by the Curators of the University of Missouri.

the authentic records of Mark Twain. His persona—often as both the protagonist *and* the narrator—is offered in a given work as an aspect of Mark Twain, or as a moment in his "life." Sometimes Mark Twain as a persona may be narrowly confined, especially in a brief journalistic piece; elsewhere he may be multifaceted, as in a sophisticated narrative like *The Innocents Abroad.* Regardless, our psychological experience in reading a Twain narrative is likely to be that we are reading a history of Mark Twain. We may be sufficiently informed to realize that such history often may not recount the life of Samuel Clemens; but, if we accept the narrative on its own terms, if we are true to the implicit contract between author and reader, then the narrative becomes part of the record of Mark Twain. Taken together, such narratives give us the fascinating story of a larger-than-life creation.

THE ABSENCE OF SAMUEL CLEMENS

The fact that the author we conceptualize is Mark Twain, not Samuel Clemens, helps explain why it is so difficult for biographers to track down Samuel Clemens through the writings of Mark Twain. Though works such as *The Innocents Abroad* and *Roughing It* originate at least partly in the experiences of Samuel Clemens, they are transmuted into narrative fiction about this other somebody named Mark Twain. Narrative, persona, and implied author are all linguistic constructs: we are persuaded to participate in the construction of the imaginary history of an imaginary being, Mark Twain, and to compose him at various periods in that history.

Even if we turn to letters, notebooks, and dictated reminiscences, we are presented with personae and authorial images that suggest Mark Twain, not Samuel Clemens. For example, in the purportedly autobiographical dictations set down in Clemens's late years, whimsy and playful exaggerations suggest more fiction and self-creation, not history— we hear the story and voice of Mark Twain, not Samuel Clemens. In the letters and notebooks, too, one senses Mark Twain much more than a flesh-and-blood man. In the process of writing, the literary consciousness, showman, and persona known as Mark Twain emerges—an intricate sensibility, a mode of thinking and expressing, a self-formed literary being. From the narratives we also construct Mark Twain, this "being" who is finally more than just an abstract or disembodied voice—a being who has become a cultural icon and stands on his own as a clearly recognizable personality, as evidenced by films such as *The Adventures of Mark Twain* and a plethora of other popular accounts of his life and times.

It's tempting to think of Mark Twain as a mask of Samuel Clemens, but that notion is misleading if we consider a mask as something static, something donned and doffed at will. There may be a great deal of Samuel Clemens in Mark Twain, though just how much we may never determine. Just as his narratives are often built on fictionalized facts, perhaps Mark Twain is an aspect, mode of thought, or "fact" of Samuel Clemens that has been fictionalized (dramatized). Like the fiction that illuminates a fact, like the birthmark in Nathaniel Hawthorne's "The Birthmark" that cannot be removed without destroying its possessor, perhaps Mark Twain is a birthmark, or rather a "thought-mark" of Samuel Clemens, essential to his expression. In any event, though Mark Twain may be ultimately a mirage, a phony, he may be . . . a *real* phony, truly expressive of puzzling—and comic—questions about the world and the self. Perhaps the best analogy is offered by [Twain's story] *No. 44, The Mysterious Stranger:* Clemens is the "waking self"; Twain is the fascinating "dream self," the creator, narrator, and protagonist of a wealth of dream adventures. Perhaps Mark Twain is Samuel Clemens rendered fantastic and glorious—or at least humorous, even in his "darkest" narratives. As long as we stay within those narratives, concerning ourselves with persona and implied author, we need not be concerned with what Samuel Clemens was "really" like—though we may occasionally wish to speculate.

PLAYFUL SUBJECTIVITY

While Twain's narratives encourage us to accept him and his adventures on their own terms, sometimes they also prompt us to question what we read. Twain's playfulness, capacity for change, and penchant for hoax may, at times, induce us to wonder in what manner a particular narrative is to be regarded. In other words, even within the context of a narrative we may be puzzled; Twain's narratives sometimes delight in undercutting themselves.

Moreover, while these narratives present Mark Twain and his (usually invented) "experiences," they nonetheless are, in a sense, often reportorial, pointing "outward." That is, they present places—the Old World, the American West—for our consideration. These places may ultimately serve as settings or backdrops for Mark Twain's comic revels, but we may still wonder just how accurately these settings are rendered. Again, Twain may prompt us to various responses: at times we may accept his descriptions, at other times we may question them. Twain seems sometimes a reporter, sometimes a dreamer. On occasion we may question whether there even *is* an "outside" or objective world (that is, a world open to *anyone's* factual portrayal). In short, just as [Herman] Melville leads us to contemplate the whiteness of the whale in *Moby-Dick* and [Edgar Allan] Poe confronts us with a snow-white "shrouded human figure" in *Pym*, Twain brings us to face a blankness, an epistemological void. Twain's method is comic rather than melodramatic or horrific; nevertheless, by encouraging us to ponder Mark Twain, his adventures, and his world, he prompts us, at least occasionally, to philosophical speculation. We may recall the mind-world or subject-object problems posted in epistemology: we are presented with a mind, Mark Twain, of whose narrative "reality" we are assured yet whose changeability may puzzle (and delight) us. We may laughingly wonder how to consider this mind, its experiences, and its relationship to any "outside" world; and thereby we may find some parallels to our own situation, as we narrate our own existence to ourselves. Twain suggests how complex and indeterminate is the relationship between mind and object, narrative and world.

Be that as it may, we enjoy Mark Twain's adventures and forms for their own sake. Mark Twain may manifest himself in various ways in a particular work, including the narrator's voice and the voices of those characters who seem to be projecting, at least partly, the implied author's views and consciousness. In his early writings Twain favors first-person narrations; thus, he may be generally identified with these narrator-protagonists, these narrative voices. Each role or voice is, in a sense, an incarnation of Mark Twain—a particular self that Twain may become, or express himself as, for the purposes of that narrative. As implied author, Twain is the inventive capacity, the creator of all these voices and selves, the containing envelope for all these particularities and aspects of himself. He gives a measure of continuity to these various narratives and lets us speak of Mark Twain generally, instead of just the Mark Twain of *The Innocents Abroad* or the Mark Twain of *Roughing It*. He lets us talk about the voices or personae *of* Mark Twain.

With each new narrative, Mark Twain is expressed in increasingly complex ways. Indeed, with the completion of *Roughing It*, Mark Twain has evolved into a multifaceted personality a bit like Harry Haller in [German author Herman] Hesse's *Steppenwolf:* a "Magic Theater" of seemingly innumerable dramatic and creative possibilities, a domain for a medley of "selves" or potentialities. Like Haller, Twain becomes a fluid consciousness that delights in dissolving distinctions, staging scenes that are simultaneously realistic and surrealistic, and expressing an array of attitudes and tones.

LIBERATION THROUGH HUMOR

The way to enter the Magic Theater of Haller's mind is through humor: Haller laughs at an image of himself in a mirror, shattering his self-image into many pieces. Thereby freed from restrictive notions of self, identity, and reality, Haller is able to enter the Magic Theater and play with the multiplicities and possibilities of his mind. So, too, does Mark Twain use humor as a liberating and volatilizing power, a comic impulse that recasts experience, world, and self into new forms. Humor is an awareness of the incongruities and multiplicities in world and self—and it is also a playful willingness to use this awareness to reshape, or view anew, world and self.

That humor depends upon a playful and pleasant awareness of incongruities and offers liberation is not a new idea, of course. In his essay "Humour" (1927) Sigmund Freud noted that "humour has something liberating about it, but it also has something of grandeur and elevation." He added:

> The grandeur of it clearly lies in the triumph of narcissism, the victorious assertion of the ego's invulnerability. The ego refuses to be distressed by the provocations of reality to let itself be compelled to suffer. It insists that it cannot be affected by the traumas of the external world; it shows, in fact, that such traumas are no more than occasions for it to gain pleasure.

Similarly, [film critic] Norman N. Holland contends that "if we perceive a sudden, playful incongruity that gratifies conscious and unconscious wishes and defeats conscious and unconscious fears to give a feeling of liberation, then we laugh." Where I differ from this well-established psychoanalytic line is in my emphasis on humor as offering volatility and creativity. Rather than seeing humor as simply reassuring the ego (or re-creating one's identity theme, as Holland would have it), I see humor—Mark Twain's humor, at any rate—as offering fluidity, expansion, and adventure, thereby engendering *new* images of world and self.

Within Twain's comic narratives, then, the world may be created afresh. By refusing to let experience dictate his role, by laughing at everyday distinctions, conventions, and fixities— by rejecting, in short, anything that might fixate him—Twain asserts through humor the variability and inventiveness that make up his persona. Humor's ability to uncover life's lurking disjunctions, ambiguities, and absurdities—life's general "messiness"—lets Twain suggest that neither world nor self is so knowable, stable, or determined as generally assumed. By denying a fixed and wholly objective world, humor frees the mind to shift ideas and perspectives easily, to revel in the exposure and creation of the absurd. Humor dissolves appearances, revealing the hidden formlessness of life in order to let the mind laughingly manufacture its own forms.

In some respects Twain uses humor the way Socrates used irony. As [Danish philosopher] Søren Kierkegaard pointed out in *The Concept of Irony*, Socrates (and later, [German philosopher Georg Wilhelm] Hegel) used irony as "infinite absolute negativity." Kierkegaard explained: "Here, then, we see irony in all its divine infinitude, which allows nothing whatever to endure." Constantly changing ironic masks, Socrates exposed human foibles and pretenses—especially the pretense that we really know the world and ourselves. Such a "clearing away" of false knowledge, such a brushfire among the thickets of illusion and conceit, enabled Socrates to indicate what was hitherto concealed: the sphere of the Absolute, the "really real" realm of Ideas.

Twain's humor also engages in this ironic dissolution of conventionally accepted "reality." As burlesque, hoax, linguistic game, or satire, Twain's multiform humor often denies the reality principle, denies the world as an objective and imposing force, and denies the power of circumstance to fix, define, or limit. Like philosophical ironists from Socrates to Kierkegaard, Twain uses his ironic humor to suggest that life is more illusory and protean than commonly believed. Kierkegaard's observation that irony grants seemingly infinite opportunities for playing with the world may be aptly applied to Twain's humorous reshaping of experience.

Twain differs from this long tradition of metaphysical irony in his refusal to espouse any absolute truth, any noumenal realm behind the phenomenal world. Whereas ironists like Socrates, Hegel, and Kierkegaard used irony to strip away veils of appearances to reveal Truth, Twain's humor strips away veils in order to suggest further veils, with existence as a shadow show. Indeed, Twain loves to destroy illusions *and* to reveal—or create—new ones in their stead. If there is anything "real" in Twain's writings, it is his creative consciousness, his power to make his own world. Absolute reality is the literary mind itself: Mark Twain as creator of selves, hoaxes, and illusions.

Mocking Reality

It is Mark Twain's humor, his exuberant transforming of experience, that reveals him to us; humor simultaneously creates, sustains, and expresses his versatile persona. As an active agent for change, humor lets him alter subject and stance at will; it grants him power and freedom. Even when narrating humiliations, he asserts through laughter his invulnerability to painful experiences, his liberation from restraint. By using the creative quirkiness of humor he links moods, events, and people in fresh and unexpected ways, presenting a world that he wants or at least can control. Mark Twain's humor is his liberating power to refashion life according to the fluidity of his own mind; it is his freedom from definitions, concrete events, and causalities. It suggests that beneath the apparently solid world is a world of sportive absurdity, a protean, unfathomable world open to continual remaking. This revelation empowers Twain to be likewise protean, creative, absurd—to remake the world and his persona within comic narrative. By volatilizing and reinventing the world, Twain's humor engenders a volatile, evolving persona. The process is interactive: By changing himself, Mark Twain changes his relationship with the world, and his images of it.

Moreover, humor is mainly verbal; it recasts world and self through language, suggesting that language itself is inherently unstable and that verbal representations of life are illusory. Because language is how the mind primarily conceptualizes the world and the self, such conceptualizations are naturally subject to distortion and transformation. By underscoring and magnifying the instabilities of language and thought, humor renders the world and the self protean. Through humor Twain implies that word and world are much more unsettled than we ordinarily realize. Ideas, categories, and distinctions—including those between the serious and the nonsensical—may dissolve easily in the flux of the humorous mind. In Twain, absurdity may penetrate the most serious subject; nonsense may commingle with the numinous.

Because Mark Twain is created and presented by the flux of comic language, he becomes as variable as the world he presents. Like that world, he becomes a protean linguistic phenomenon. As persona, as voice and protagonist in his narratives, he becomes as versatile as the comic words that create him. In short, Mark Twain, his writings, and his world all depend upon the versatility of his humor.

The extreme versatility of Twain's humor helps suggest why conventional explanations of humor or laughter often fail when applied to Twain's writing. For instance, [French philosopher] Henri Bergson's theory that we laugh at a lack of emotion and "mechanical inelasticity" (or "something mechanical encrusted on the living") may not explain why we laugh at Twain's humorous narratives, which often are emotionally charged and depend on flexibility, not inflexibility. To take a quick example, Twain's hilarious portrayal of himself in *The Innocents Abroad* as weeping over the alleged grave of Adam is implicitly charged with contempt for superstition and plays brilliantly and agilely off the Adam myth. Scholars such as James M. Cox and Bruce Michelson note that Twain's humor tends to be good-natured play, an act of spontaneous, childlike creation.

In *Homo Ludens* [Dutch historian] Johan Huizinga defines play as a game with its own rules, play area, and rituals; role-playing is a prominent form of play. Clearly Twain's humor often depends upon roles, masks, and games; play theory is especially applicable to *Tom Sawyer* and similar works, and much of Twain's humor can be broadly characterized as "playful." Furthermore, whether it is Cox emphasizing Freud's pleasure principle or Michelson emphasizing a sense of fun, such critics are right to point to the sheer enjoyment found in Twain's humor—a seemingly obvious fact that is occasionally overlooked in the all-too-serious world of literary scholarship.

But a preoccupation with play per se will not capture the full range of Twain's humor and persona, unless we recognize that Twain's "play" is frequently not ritualistic, not concerned with rules (which Twain tends to dissolve as soon as he makes them), and not entirely devoted to pleasure or fun. A surcharge of emotion and ideas often gives his humor a forcefulness, an ability to break down and rearrange our conceptions of the world, that is not found in play alone. For Twain, "play" is the humorous transformation of life—including all of its "rules"—into fantasy, where concepts may be set in startlingly new contexts. Moreover, Twain often gives a sense of movement, even transcendence, that is not captured by play theory, though Huizinga does include a vague feeling of "rapture" as among the "elements proper to play."

TRANSCENDENCE THROUGH HUMOR

At its best, Mark Twain's humor is both a resilient response to an incongruous world and a surmounting of that world through his ability to make his own imaginative worlds. Twain fashions worlds full of exaggerations, linguistic revels, and radically altered perceptions. The product is humorous "fantasy"; yet, as created mental realms, Twain's worlds are also "real," often containing important insights into the way in which the mind produces its sense of existence. To put it another way, Twain's humor offers both paradox and transcendence: his humor points to—and even exaggerates—the absurdities, contradictions, and illusions inherent in life, yet suggests that one can rise above life's limitations through a humorous consciousness that manufactures its own sense of life, its own place. In a world of illusions one can at least make one's *own* illusions—fantasies that are created rather than accepted, fantasies that at least have the "reality" of one's own mind. In Twain's narratives, conventional distinctions between illusion and reality are often dissolved in his expanding consciousness. Through humor Mark Twain becomes a personality whose essence or meaning rests not upon the accidents of an external world but upon itself—a literary consciousness that creates itself and is its own world.

This is not to say that the man Samuel Clemens did not face various exigencies. His literary career, especially in its early stages, was influenced by market pressures, the demands of journalism, and awareness of his various audiences. Nevertheless, Mark Twain increasingly presents himself in his narratives as a literary personality who, however fallible or self-disparaging, is largely self-made: a multifaceted, inventive (and invented) being that humorously observes—and shapes—his world. Furthermore, as he gains characteristics, stances, and voices, Mark Twain develops his own dynamic, his own motive force, which will lead him (albeit in willful and meandering ways!) through future narratives. In short, although Mark Twain obviously depends upon the experiences of Samuel Clemens, he also becomes a self-defined persona inhabiting and reveling in various literary realms.

Granted, Twain uses humor to reveal incongruities and frustrations inherent in life and in oneself—the dilemma of a sensitive being who discovers that the world is not always set up for his accommodation and that he is not always set up for his accommodation, either. Torn by conflicting desires, one needs imaginative renewal and a balance of perspectives. Twain's humor confers needed reassurance and control. It matters little if the material of humor is often discomfort, deception, or human frailty, so long as the sense of mastery remains. The inventive capability of comic narrative suggests that the locus of meaning, of reality, ultimately resides in the literary mind itself, not in the external world; it is this exuberant sense of power to reshape or resignify oneself and one's world that grants the humorist his aura of transcendence. It is not transcendence in the sense of ascending into some immortal, Platonic realm of the Absolute; rather, it is transcendence over the fears, stupidities, and general dullness of everyday life. By denying the power of the concrete world to make and define him, Mark Twain asserts his ability to form models of life—and of himself—according to his own humorous imagination.

Befitting the protean persona it helps to make and empower, Mark Twain's humor is kaleidoscopic, embodying frontier fantasy, burlesque, anecdote, cracker-box philosophy, hoax, satire, irony, literary comedy and linguistic games, and absurdity—all methods of recasting or restaging the world according to stage manager Twain's theater of moods and ideas. Despite its extreme range, Twain's humor is, at its best, a harmonizing force, balancing illusion against illusion, model against model, making a comic symphony (if occasionally out of tune) of his variegated persona. Twain presents humor as a peculiar form of music, as opposed to the discord of tragedy; the humorist delights in each tone of life and imagination. Humor lets him move almost musically from one view, role, or "self" to the next, enjoying each in its turn. Whereas tragedy tends to fixate on one problem or perspective, Twain's humor moves through a medley of moods and motifs. Even in the form of hoax or satire, jarring our beliefs and pretensions, his humor happily expresses the power of persona, his delight in playing with ideas.

In his desire to make humor, to exercise mastery, Twain often destroys models of reality that others take for granted. He frequently transgresses ordinary boundaries, habits of thought, and conceptions of life; his humor is often manifest in dreams or dreamlike scenes, power fantasies, and a persistent sense of wild, if troubled, freedom. As he constructs models of life to suit his own humorous will, Twain develops his persona. Even when exposing life's disappointments and his own flaws, Twain implicitly asserts his power to reflect upon and surmount them, to give birth to yet other—and better—selves. Ultimately Twain's humor is not of the world but of himself—a reflection of his own versatile mind, playing at increasingly higher levels. He uses humor to remake language, narrative, history, and even basic conceptions of reality and identity. He subsumes and shapes more and more of the world, making fresh associations and images. He makes humor out of the very nature of consciousness. For Twain, to think is to be humorous, to be playfully cognizant of the fluidity, nonsense, and creativity that is consciousness. Through humor Twain dreams better worlds and better selves.

Constructing a Persona for Posterity

Alan Gribben

In the following essay, Alan Gribben notes that
Samuel Clemens once attempted to write a book
based on the experiences of a man he had hired to
travel on his behalf. Though Clemens claimed to
have intended to clarify in the book that the experiences remembered therein were not really his own,
this incident provides valuable insight into the way
he cultivated the persona of his alter-ego, Mark
Twain, in his fiction. Fictionalized accounts of Mark
Twain's life—particularly those of his boyhood in
Hannibal—formed the basis of his celebrated public
image, and Clemens guarded this image jealously
throughout his career. Clemens denied for many
years the requests of those who wished to write his
official biography, and sought through legal means
to prevent the publication of unofficial biographies.
During his final years, however, Clemens grew increasingly concerned that his creation would not long endure after
his death. Seeking to forestall the publication of posthumous
biographies, Clemens permitted noted biographer Albert
Bigelow Paine to write his life story. Clemens succeeded in
galvanizing Mark Twain's public image by dictating to Paine
a largely fictitious account of his life. Alan Gribben is the author of *Mark Twain's Library: A Reconstruction.*

Precisely what is the legend about Mark Twain that enrap-
tured [Twain biographer] Albert Bigelow Paine and still in-
fatuates us? That a poor Midwestern boy masters steamboat
piloting, then proceeds to write articulately about the scenes
and attitudes of nearly every part of his homeland and many
regions of England, Europe, and the Middle East—retiring
in a magnificent Italian-style villa in the hills of Connecticut,

Excerpted from "Autobiography as Property: Mark Twain and His Legend," by Alan
Gribben, in *The Mythologizing of Mark Twain*, edited by Sara deSaussure Davis and
Philip D. Beidler. Copyright © 1984 by The University of Alabama Press. Reprinted by
permission of the University of Alabama Press.

his name to be familiar to his countrymen and foreigners alike for generations to come. This approximates the pattern of Horatio Alger tales, but in Twain's variant the protagonist smiles through tears and succeeds so gloriously that his enemies are devoured by envy. He can do something well. He has won a triumph, learning from setbacks. Whether he has been victimized by a Mexican plug horse or an unscrupulous merchant, he exaggerates his bitterness so ludicrously that we laugh. He boasts outrageously—in *A Tramp Abroad,* of his supposedly hard work in rafting, mountain climbing, hotel visiting. And he never takes too seriously his association with so many famous people of his day. Irreverent humor will triumph effortlessly, he seems to claim, provided that we remember how ridiculous and credulous is the mass of humanity.

Clemens passed his final years shaping and adjusting the image he hoped to leave behind, utilizing each newspaper and magazine interview. When he died, he was mourned by every section of the United States, for he had linked himself with most parts of the nation (except Florida, the Pacific Northwest, and Texas), becoming an American of no particular region, erasing his regionalism rather than emphasizing it. He had stayed long enough to master various new environments, then moved on, moving West (like the imagination of the country), and at last returning East to report and reminisce. He left behind an identity with each region, and the inhabitants thanked him for making their humdrum existence seem novel and amusing. (Twain established more regional identities than Harriet Beecher Stowe, citizen of Ohio, Maine, Connecticut, Florida; George Washington Cable, who combined Louisiana and Massachusetts; John Steinbeck, of California and New York City; Neil Simon, the East Coast, the West Coast, the desert Southwest. Twain had the Mississippi River Valley, from Muscatine to New Orleans; Nevada and California; the city of Buffalo; New England and Hartford; the European continent, especially England, Germany, France, Switzerland, and Austria; New York City; and finally Redding, Connecticut.)

As a result of Clemens' intention to surpass rivals such as Bret Harte in future acclaim as well as present-day sales, and his anxiety about his lack of formal education, he came to value every morsel, every scrap, every particle of his life, placing a mercenary price on each incident and episode as they befell him. His biographical experiences were viewed the same way he had seen men in Nevada and California approach those inert, lucrative mountains: he intended to work them like a paying ore mine; his life was a lode, vein, grubstake, payload, tracer, unpanned claim, bonanza. His determined attitude resembled his literary advice to William Wright, known as Dan De Quille, when the latter was undertaking a book about the Western mines: "I'll show you how to make a man read every one of those sketches, under the stupid impression that they are mere accidental incidents that have dropped in on you unawares in the course of your *narrative.*"

GUARDING HIS LIFE HISTORY

Twain's terrific possessiveness about his posthumous image was no more fierce than his proprietary feelings about personal manuscripts and letters. Even the methodical autograph hunter was, in his words, "another phase of human depravity" (New York *Herald*, 20 January 1901). On 19 October 1865, in the famous letter that Clemens wrote to his brother and sister-in-law from San Francisco, he acknowledged that he was yielding to "a 'call' to literature of a low order—i.e., humorous. It is nothing to be proud of, but it is my strongest suit." He added a postscript (futilely, as it proved) that same night: "P.S. You had better shove this in the stove—for . . . I don't want any absurd 'literary remains' & 'unpublished letters of Mark Twain' published after I am planted." To Orion Clemens he boasted in 1887: "I have never yet allowed an interviewer or biography-sketcher to get out of me any circumstance of my history which I thought might be worth putting some day into my autobiography. . . . I hate all public mention of my private history, anyway. It is none of the public's business. . . . I have been approached as many as five hundred times on the biographical-sketch lay, but they never got anything that was worth the printing." This point of view was hardly unique to Clemens, of course. One of Clemens' most admired poets, Rudyard Kipling, refused a request to cooperate with a biography of his aunt, Lady Burne-Jones, explaining: "My objection stands, tho' it be a selfish one. I'm too fond of her, and loved her too much in my childhood and youth, to share my feelings with *any* public. This here biography and 'reminiscer' business that is going on nowadays is a bit too near the Higher Cannibalism to please me. Ancestor-worship is all right, but serving them up filleted, or spiced or 'high' (which last is very popular) has put me off."

After a man named Will M. Clemens published *Mark Twain: His Life and Work* in 1892, he had the audacity to write to the celebrated man with whom he shared a name, but no kinship, requesting permission to publish *The Mark Twain Story Book*, "The Homes and Haunts of Mark Twain," and a biographical sketch. Clemens replied with acerbity on 6 June 1900: "I am sorry to object, but I really must. Such books as you propose are not proper to publish during my lifetime. A man's history *is his own property* until the grave extinguishes his ownership in it. I am strenuously opposed to having books of a biographical character published about me while I am still alive." This sense of his autobiographical details as a form of property infused his attitudes throughout the remainder of his life, and can be detected in the letter he wrote to Henry H. Rogers, seeking legal assistance from his Standard Oil patron: "Here is this troublesome cuss, Will M. Clemens, turning up again. I won't have it . . . . Watch for advertisements of these books . . . so that you can set Wilder or some other brisk lawyer to work squashing them at the right time. . . . [Will] Clemens can't write books—he is a mere maggot who tries to feed on people while they are still alive." Unavailingly, Will Clemens tried to argue the point further: "In no instance have I or would I copy a single line of your copyrighted work. But your public spoken utterances become public property once they are spoken and there is no law against writing truthful facts concerning a man's life. The book is shelved for the moment much to my regret and loss—I can wait."

RETURNING TO HANNIBAL

Aware that aggravating meddlers like Will Clemens were lurking in the wings, Samuel Clemens faced his dwindling years with concern about what might happen once he was incapacitated, rendered helpless to affect the outcome. At least there was consolation in the fact that he had long promoted his many books as making up the record of his life. One manifestation of this effort, *Mark Twain's Library of Humor* (1888), edited by Clemens in collaboration with William Dean Howells and Charles Hopkins Clark, included a headnote to the first selection from each humorist's writings. Mark Twain's own introduction, printed above "The

Notorious jumping Frog," reads:

> Samuel L. Clemens (Mark Twain) was born at Hannibal, Mo.,
> in 1835, and after serving an apprenticeship to the printing
> business in his brother's office there, "learned the river," as
> pilot. . . . His earliest book, 'The Innocents Abroad," was the
> result of his experience and observation as a passenger on
> the *Quaker City* in her famous cruise to the Holy Land. His
> succeeding books *continue the story of his own life,* with more
> or less fullness and exactness. After his return from Palestine,
> he was for a year in Buffalo, N.Y., but has ever since lived in
> Hartford, Conn. [italics added]. . .

Viewed chronologically, Twain's travel narratives, novels,
short stories, sketches, essays, and speeches take up the
events of his life in a curious order, skipping from recent
episodes to earliest ones, then returning to later incidents,
then intermixing them almost capriciously, as though linear
time narrative had no validity, making the phases of his life
the apparent jumble that both *Mark Twain's Library of Humor* and his autobiographical dictations—two literary productions that he controlled entirely—turned out to be.
Clemens and his commentators were correct in noting that
the story of his life was in his books, but the order of narration is far from uniform or predictable. "The Turning Point of
My Life" (1910), for example, an essay searching for cause-
and-effect occurrences in his boyhood, appeared during his
final months. Beginning in 1876, however, one feature became consistent: Mark Twain recurrently returned to what
[Twain biographer] Henry Nash Smith has labeled "The Matter of Hannibal," or what in the popular imagination might be
called "The Adventures of Mark Twain," after the books and
film by that title. As [literary scholar] Larzer Ziff has commented, "He . . . visualized his career as an ellipse that would
turn and turn again past the town rather than as a steady
movement out-ward. . . . Formed by the drowsing river town,
Mark Twain held steadily in his career to the community of
his adolescence." Though he never went back to Hannibal to
live "he always remained in orbit around its values. . . . [He]
had] a belief in experience as valuable to the extent that the
town recognizes its distinction and admires it."

It is worthwhile to be reminded that Clemens did not arrive at a full appreciation of the appeal of "the story of his
own life" all at once, and that he failed to recognize the material that ultimately gave him his greatest fame and fur-
nished the revered aspects of his Mississippi River back-

ground, until he was more than forty years of age, and only after other writers—particularly Thomas Bailey Aldrich in *The Story of a Bad Boy* (1869)—had preceded him in various ways and had supplied him with usable examples. In "The Celebrated Jumping Frog" (1865) he recounted a mining-camp experience that presumably happened lately; in *Innocents Abroad* (1869) a voyage from which the correspondent-vandal had just returned; in *Roughing It* (1872) a Far West saga already in danger of losing its credibility; in *The Gilded Age* (1873) a steamboat explosion, a Missouri village, and the Washington scene; in "Old Times" (1875) a cub pilot's narrative of long-past history; at last, in *Tom Sawyer* (1876), the escapades of boys who swam in the Mississippi River before the Civil War.

Though this autobiographical impulse of Mark Twain is a characteristic strain in American literature, nonetheless, current literary criticism regularly berates the attention to Samuel Clemens' personal life that dilutes so many serious interpretations of his writings. Obviously the man and the works can scarcely be separated without tremendous, premeditated effort. Moreover, this notion of synonymity between Twain and his writings is hardly new. A Princeton professor of English observed in 1904:

> The autobiographic element in the work of Mark Twain has often been pointed out, but it is not perhaps generally realized that the interest of his books varies directly in proportion to the presence of this personal element. . . . He is at his best when he is recording his own experiences: and in his happiest vein when he is transfusing them into a work of art, as in his crowning achievements of *Tom Sawyer* and *Huckleberry Finn*. And this is because his life itself has been typically— one might almost say, uniquely—American. . . . We hardly need the author's assurance that most of the adventures in *Tom Sawyer* really occurred, for the story breathes conviction from every page. The scenes in the schoolroom, the Sunday-school, and the village church reproduce for us the atmosphere of the little inland town as persuasively as Mr. Aldrich's *Bad Boy* does that of old New England.

Seeking a Stand-In

Yet sometimes a single lifetime seemed insufficient to Clemens. He mastered the craft of writing books so adroitly that he could barely reclaim autobiographical materials rapidly enough to keep his machinelike pen in operation. He began to long for a Clemens-clone, or at least a remote-controlled robot recorder. This fantasy first became explicit in his letter (written from Buffalo on 28 November 1870) to his publisher Elisha Bliss: "I have put my greedy hands on the best man in America for my purpose and shall *start him to the diamond fields of South Africa within a fortnight, at my expense.* I shall write a book of his experiences for next spring, . . . and write it just as if I had been through it all myself, but will explain in the preface that this is done merely to give it life and reality. . . . This thing is brim-full of fame and fortune for both author and publisher."

The victim-beneficiary of this scheme was James H. Riley, a veteran of mining camps in California, Mexico, and Central America, whom Clemens had known in Washington, where Riley had become a clerk to several U.S. senators. Clemens persuaded Riley to leave for the diamond fields by promising to pay him $100 a month and his passage to South Africa. Riley could collect up to $5,000 worth of diamonds, but above that amount he must send half the profits to his patron. He was to keep detailed diaries of his months of prospecting and then consent to live in Clemens' house for up to a year, "for, the purpose of your diary is to keep *you* . . . bright and inspire your tongue every morning when you take a seat in my study. You are to talk one or two hours to me every day, and *tell* your story." Clemens liked to joke that Jules Verne had in effect dispatched his doppelgänger to collect adventures in remote, dangerous regions. To Riley he explained: "I should write this book as if *I* went through all these adventures myself—this in order to give it snap and freshness. But would begin the book by saying: 'When Daniel de Foe wanted to know what life on a solitary island was like, and doubted whether he was hardy enough to stand it himself, he sent the ingenious Robinson W. Crusoe; and when I wanted to know all about wild life in the diamond fields and its fascinations, and could not go myself, I sent the ingenious Riley.'" Like Clemens' typesetter venture, this South African pipe dream had some basis in reality: there was a genuine possibility that American readers would have relished a firsthand account of the scramble for precious gems. And whereas [Ottmar] Mergenthaler's Linotype invention would eclipse Clemens' typesetting machine, another African exploit began unfolding simultaneously with Clemens' brainstorm about the diamond fields, a journalism stunt destined to place the words "Dr. Livingstone, I presume?" in history books. By a coincidence that points up how unerringly Clemens' hunches anticipated and paralleled events that made other people famous, in the previous year (1869) newspaper editor James Gordon Bennett had secretly commissioned Henry M. Stanley to penetrate central Africa and find David Livingstone as a scoop for the New York *Herald.* Stanley started his expedition on 21 March 1871 and reached Livingstone on 10 November 1871. But Clemens' South Africa enterprise merely illustrated the unpredictability of human affairs: James Riley, who yielded to Clemens' blandishments, became gravely ill before he and Clemens could commence the proposed schedule of dictations, and this defective other self died in 1872. Clemens, grudgingly, had to reimburse the American Publishing Company for $2,000, money optimistically advanced to the ill-fated Riley.

AUTOBIOGRAPHY AS FICTION

The linchpin of Clemens' interpretation of his life was the series of autobiographical dictations he left behind to forestall unauthorized versions of his legend. He labored on these in earnest during the final six years of his life, especially in 1906 and 1907. From the first, he claimed to have discovered a new freedom of expression in their uncensored, conversational form. On 10 January 1906 Clemens observed, in his Autobiographical Dictation, that "an autobiography that leaves out the little things and enumerates only the big ones is no proper picture of the man's life at all." These minor incidents would constitute what [American historian] Henry Adams once called a "shield of protection in the grave," a way to "take your own life . . . in order to prevent biographers from taking it in theirs." He could say anything he wished here, Clemens gloated. He could speak of foreign missionary work as "that least excusable of all human trades."

He would have concurred with William Sydney Porter (O. Henry), who declared in 1909 or 1910: "I do not remember ever to have read an autobiography, a biography, or a piece of fiction that told the *truth.* Of course, I have read such stuff as [French philosopher Jean Jacques] Rousseau and [French writer Émile] Zola and [Irish writer] George Moore; and various memoirs that were supposed to be window panes in their respective breasts; but mostly, all of them were either liars, actors, or poseurs. . . . The trouble about writing the truth has been that the writers . . . were trying either to do a piece of immortal literature, or to shock the public or to please editors. Some of them succeeded in all three, but they did not write the *truth*." [Fellow writer William D.] Howells had indicated mild skepticism in a well-known letter of 14 February 1904: "I'd like immensely to read your autobiography," he wrote to Clemens. "I fancy you may tell the truth about yourself. But *all* of it? . . . Even *you* won't tell the black heart's-truth. The man who could do it would be famed to the last day the sun shone on."

PRESERVING MARK TWAIN'S IMAGE AFTER HIS DEATH

Margalit Fox is a writer for The New York Times. *In the following excerpt from one of her articles, Fox discusses Mark Twain's daughter Clara Clemens's efforts during the years following her father's death to preserve his carefully constructed image.*

After her father died in 1910, [Mark Twain's daughter Clara] fought vigorously to suppress writings by or about him that she deemed inconsistent with his wholesome image. One of Twain's literary executors, Bernard DeVoto, resigned after Clara suppressed his edition of Twain's bitter 1909 polemic, "Letters From the Earth," which dealt bluntly with questions of religion and human sexuality. (The work was eventually published shortly before Clara's death in 1962). And for "Mark Twain and the Happy Island," a 1913 book about Twain's visits to Bermuda, she forbade the author, Elizabeth Wallace, to publish any photos depicting Twain with his Angelfish Club, a group of pretty young girls with whom he corresponded in the last years of his life.

Margalit Fox, "Putting a Happy Face on an Often Unhappy Twain," the *New York Times*, April 22, 2000.

Assuredly, Clemens' autobiographical dictations are no standard collection of polite character sketches, but their "truth" is scarcely an issue. They form a labyrinthian exploration of his fictionalizing genius, introducing as many foes as friends, less interested in properly recording history than in giving his version of it a liveliness that is impossible either to contravene or to resist. He skimps most on those incidents concerning illustrious personages that received the chief attention in the earlier memoirs of Howells and [writer] Andrew D. White and other works he respected—meetings with social lions and celebrated authors—and emphasizes instead the shouted insult of [childhood friend] Tom Nash, the chicanery of publishers and business associates, the random conversation with a passing acquaintance. However, Albert Bigelow Paine noted insightfully: "The things he told of Mrs. Clemens and of [his daughter] Susy were true—marvelously and beautifully true, in spirit and in aspect—and the actual detail of these mattered little in such a record. The rest was history only as *Roughing It* is history, or the *Tramp Abroad;* that is to say, it was fictional history, with fact as a starting-point." "We were watching," wrote Paine of those open-air dictating sessions, "one of the great literary creators of his time in the very process of his architecture."

TWO MARK TWAINS

There were two Mark Twains, as it turned out: the affable St. Petersburg-Tom Sawyerish-Mississippi River cub pilot, and the raging autobiographical dictation curmudgeon who now erupted daily. Perversely, Twain would have it that both impressions should be left behind for later ages to reconcile, if possible. Today it seems as though, in the latter mood, Clemens viewed himself as a potential Émile Zola in those unpopular crusades against Belgian and American imperialism, [U.S. Army General Frederick] Funston, missionaries, and other professions and personalities; he had been much impressed with Zola's "J'Accuse!," which had appeared in a Paris journal in January 1898 while Clemens was living in Vienna.

The reactions of the modern age to Clemens' heresies have been more accommodating than he could have envisioned. Van Wyck Brooks phrased it succinctly in *The Ordeal of Mark Twain:* "He was irritable, but literary men are always supposed to be that; he was old, and old people are often afflicted with doubts about the progress and welfare of mankind; he had a warm and tender heart, an abounding scorn of humbug."

The aging Clemens, contemplating his place in the annals of American literature, culture, and history, had mentioned in a letter of the 1900s to his daughter Clara: "I go out frequently and exhibit my clothes. Howells has dubbed me the 'Whited Sepulchre.' Yes, dear child, I'm a 'recognized immortal genius' and a most dissipated one too." Clara added that her father "was now so generally recognized by everyone on the street or in public places that it was difficult to realize he was only a man of letters. Sometimes he was greeted by applause when he entered a theater or public dining-room."

And yet after 1904 Clemens had no living wife to write a memoir like *Crowding Memories,* as Mrs. Thomas Bailey Aldrich loyally did; his only relative with literary inclinations, Samuel Moffett, drowned in 1908. After 1909, in fact, Clemens had no close relative, except one songstress daughter. Toward the end of his life, Clemens merely had a reliable publisher, Harper and Brothers, which was expertly guided in its decisions by Frederick Duneka; a trustworthy authorized biographer, Albert Bigelow Paine; and, until 1909, a devoted private secretary, Isabel V. Lyon. With these resources Clemens faced the future void. He had tried to establish the so-called "story of his own life" in numerous travel narratives and novels, and he would release selected excerpts from his autobiographical dictations. Then, finally, there would be that (lately discovered) self-justifying, malicious letter Clemens wrote to Howells about Isabel Lyon's character and behavior. He could also benefit from the autobiographical writings of Howells and White and others, such as Benjamin Franklin and [Italian sculptor] Benvenuto Cellini, who had demonstrated methods of prefabricating one's professional reputation and personal memorial. Here were stratagems to keep one from vanishing without residual honor and affection, the fate of talented men like [writer] A.D. Richardson and [humorist] Artemus Ward.

Understandably, Clemens' confidence deserted him at the end. Clara recalled that, during his final illness, "he appeared skeptical . . . as to whether the sale of his books would continue for more than a brief period after his death," and he told Clara he regretted not leaving behind more money. Only a few months later, in 1911, the executors of the estate dispersed much of his private library at an urgent sale in New York City, as though intending to capitalize on what could be fleeting fame, but they need not have rushed. As [Twain biographer] Justin Kaplan remarks, he bequeathed us "a legendary life and a dazzling presence, one of the shaping styles of America's literature and thought, half a dozen of its major books, and . . . in the end Mark Twain is more imposing than the sum of his work." Clemens, "a genius at generating publicity, had created Mark Twain, a public figure recognizable on almost any street in America." Every passing decade further blurs the distinctions between Samuel L. Clemens and his better-known alter ego. It can now be recognized that, mixed in with his many books, was another supremely self-conscious work of art, Mark Twain's enduring legend.

CHAPTER 3

Mark Twain's Career

MARK TWAIN

What's Funny About Mark Twain?

William Baker

In the following essay, William Baker evaluates
those qualities of Mark Twain's literary humor that
earned him the distinction of being America's fore-
most humorist. Baker suggests that highly irreverent,
exaggeration-laden humor had long been a well-
established storytelling technique among American
humorists before Mark Twain employed it in his
writing. So too, Baker notes, had humorists already
underscored the comic aspects of their literary per-
sonas by contrasting them with serious, "straight-
man" characters before Twain's appearance in
American letters. Nor, Baker asserts, was Twain's
prominence as a humorist the result of particularly
innovative or unique subject matter. Rather, Baker
suggests, what distinguished Twain's work from that
of his fellow humorists was three specific literary
effects applied so uniquely and effectively by Twain
that one can identify his literary works by their presence. William Baker is a professor of English at
Wright State University.

What's funny? We Americans, an odd lot, can't easily explain
what tickles our personal funny bones. Mark Twain tickles
me all over the place. Often a single word dropped into the
right sentence at the right time—"a solitary esophagus slept
upon motionless wing" for example—will send me into
howls of laughter. But what kills *me*—those esophagus
words—would mean little in a list by themselves, so a search
for Twain's essence will need to go beyond the esophagus.

Mark Twain used humor to illuminate character and to
teach lessons about humanity—a technique of the moralist
at least as old as the Bible. But risibility is not morality. And

Reprinted, by permission of the author, from "What's Funny About Mark Twain?" by
William Baker, *Mark Twain Journal*, vol. 21, no. 4 (Fall 1985), pp. 5–7.

since his subject matter covered everything under the sun, his humor must come from means, not matter. I think a special Twain quality exists in that means. Since earlier Americans had popularized our peculiarly national humor—lethal doses of irreverence and oceans of exaggeration—we can't say they are special to Twain, even though he used them to perfection. So, it must be his manner—his posture and the unique effects he created—that makes his particular laughter machine work so well.

By posture I mean that his masks (or alternate personae) allowed Twain (a mask for Clemens) to create foils, that is, characters who could say what Sam could not. He could introduce his foils in standard English and often in a dead pan mask and then let them earn their keep in the vernacular of the river, the mines, the print shop, the newspaper office, the poker game, or even Wall Street.

Still the mask or foil was not unique to Twain, and so we must look closely at his special effects for his essence. Three particular effects he used, effects so transformed by him that we can examine almost any humorous story of his era and detect whether his hand was in it, are "substituting," "bubbling along," and (less frequently) "cartooning." Please note I said "almost"; no system is perfect.

"SUBSTITUTING" AND "BUBBLING ALONG"

By "substituting" I mean using an unexpected word or phrase for one that is anticipated. Substitution provides juxtaposition of intention, as in the esophagus example. The last thing we would expect to see sweeping along on "motionless wing" is an esophagus. Twain says, "When I was a young man I studied for the *gallows*." We expect a word like *law* or *business,* and we are startled and amused by the substitute, *gallows*. "Ignorant people," says Twain (to cite another illustration) "think it's the noise which fighting cats make that is so aggravating, but it ain't so; it's the sickening grammar they use."

"Bubbling along" is defined in Twain's "How To Tell a Story."

> The humorous story is American, the comic story is English, the witty story is French. The humorous story depends for its effect upon the *manner* of the telling; the comic story and the witty story upon the *matter*.

> The humorous story may be spun out to great length, and

may wander around as much as it pleases, and arrive nowhere in particular; but the comic and witty stories must be brief and end with a point. The humorous story bubbles along, the others burst.

The humorous story is strictly a work of art—high and delicate art—and only an artist can tell it; but no art is necessary in telling the comic and the witty story; anybody can do it. The art of telling a humorous story—understand, I mean by word of mouth, not print—was created in America, and has remained at home.

Twain makes "bubbling along" seem like an easy journey from New York to Boston, drifting gently by way of Chicago, New Orleans, and San Francisco. It is much more than that. It is the fecund inventiveness, the veritable cascade of ideas tumbling one after another—indeed the fertile intellectual productivity inside the "bubbling along" that sets Twain apart.

Consider the coyote episode from *Roughing It*. The coyote is described fully and we think there is nothing more a sane man would reveal about the "sorry-looking skeleton, with a gray wolf-skin stretched over it." A casual observation is made: "If you start a swift-footed dog after him, you will enjoy it ever so much—especially if it is a dog that has a good opinion of himself and has been brought up to believe he knows something about speed." Now we follow that dog in his pursuit of the coyote and see Twain's fecundity at work. A reasonable man would simply say, "The dog could never catch the coyote," but Twain pushes the idea and lets it bubble along, until through our tears of laughter we think—and we hope—that his fecundity will be infinite. Even the "and . . . and . . . and" construction of the sentences conveys an "on to infinity" idea:

The coyote will go swinging gently off on that deceitful trot of his, and every little while he will smile a fraudful smile over his shoulder that will fill that dog entirely full of encouragement and worldly ambition, and make him lay his head still lower to the ground, and stretch his neck further to the front, and pant more fiercely, and stick his tail out straighter behind, and move his furious legs with a yet wilder frenzy, and leave a broader and broader, and higher and denser cloud of desert sand smoking behind, and marking his long wake across the level plain! And all this time the dog is only a short twenty feet behind the coyote, and to save the soul of him he cannot understand why it is that he cannot get perceptibly closer; and he begins to get aggravated, and it makes him madder and madder to see how gently the coyote glides along and never pants or sweats or ceases to smile; and he grows still more and more incensed to see how shamefully he has been taken in by an entire stranger, and what an ignoble swindle that long, calm, soft-footed trot is; and next he notices that he is getting fagged, and that the coyote actually has to slacken speed a little to keep from running away from him—and *then* that towndog is mad in earnest, and he begins to strain and weep and swear, and paw the sand higher than ever, and reach for the coyote with concentrated and desperate energy. This "spurt" finds him six feet behind the gliding enemy, and two miles from his friends. And then, in the instant that a wild new hope is lighting up his face, the coyote turns and smiles blandly upon him once more, and with a something about it which seems to say: "Well, I shall have to tear myself away from you, bub—business is business, and it will not do for me to be fooling along this way all day"—and forthwith there is a rushing sound, and the sudden splitting of a long crack through the atmosphere, and behold that dog is solitary and alone in the midst of a vast solitude!

I submit that the quality of the work here was not only new on the American scene, but it is the essence of Twain's humor. Who else could have written it?

BUILDING HUMOROUS TENSION

The bubbling-along effect stemmed from Twain's experience as a speaker. He noticed that his greatest laughs came after a series of more or less minor amusements. Therefore he became master of the pause. Tell a joke. Wait for the laugh. The wait, he said in his memoirs, was more important than the joke. Tell a related joke. Wait again. The audience laughs and is ready to move on. Surely he cannot top the second. And then he does! Out comes the related third joke and the audience shouts and howls. The third is unexpected, and, usually, of course, carefully edited to be the best, and the audience not only finds itself amazed at his inventiveness but also surprised to find itself laughing for a third time—surprised and delighted.

The controlled exasperation of Scotty the miner and the minister fresh from the East in "Buck Fanshaw's Funeral" kills us, but its subtleness allows the reader to watch the characters fire off cannon-balls of language at close range and miss completely. As readers we stand outside the window, looking into the room. The minister has to wait for three euphemisms ("gone up the flume," "throwed up the sponge," "kicked the bucket") before he becomes aware of Scotty's mission. And the humor is intensified by the minister's own euphemism (from *Hamlet*) "Ah—has departed to that mysterious country from whose bourne no traveler returns." Scotty pounces on the one word he understands and says, "Return! I reckon not. Why pard, he's dead!" And we have finally come to the plain English of it.

End of humor? Of course not. Twain has become enamored of the idea and plays on, like a juggler who begins with three balls and keeps adding and adding and adding until we are astonished at ten balls floating in front of our eyes. Scotty and the minister keep missing each other as they bubble along. We realize of course that even a minister new to the West couldn't be that stupid and that Scotty—for all his plainness—seems to be putting the minister on. But having gotten into the story we are quite content—such has been the skill of the juggler—to suspend our disbelief and wade through our tears of laughter to the end.

The story is funny because the roles are juxtaposed, because the level of exasperation is intense, and because it treats a sober and profound subject—death—with lightness and jocularity. It also clashes two distinct dialects, but what makes it funniest, I think, is the effect I mentioned earlier—fecund inventiveness. Call it piling on. Scotty keeps baffling the minister long after the first clash of the dialects.

Twain enthusiasts will wonder if Clemens wasn't thinking of "His Grandfather's Old Ram" (Chapter 53 of *Roughing It*), when he mentioned bubbling along, and while he may well have been, I am using the term in a slightly different sense, as I will try to show. Jim Blaine tells of his grandfather bending over to pick up a dime, his back to the ram, with Smith of Calavaras watching; no it was Smith of Tulare; no it was Smith of Sacramento, who married a Whitaker, who gave a glass eye to Flora Ann Baxter, who married a Hagadorn, who was eaten by cannibals, but not by accident, as the example of his Uncle Lem's dog shows, a dog he got from Wheeler, who was caught up in the machinery of the carpet factory. Since we never hear what happened to the ram, the story is a successful exercise in sustained suspense, and is, in fact, a hoax on the reader. Fecund inventiveness is used to distract and distance the reader from the ram, not as I have suggested in other examples, in the spinning out of a single idea.

Twain's inventiveness was not only verbal; it sometimes had a visual or cartooning quality as well. He seemed to be inventing moving cartoons several decades before Krazy Kat

(1913) and almost a century before Bugs Bunny or the Road-runner. A cartoon effect occurs in the coyote episode previously cited. When we read "forthwith there is a rushing sound, and the sudden splitting of a long crack through the atmosphere, and behold that dog is solitary and alone in the midst of a vast solitude," we think immediately of the movie cartoon of the Roadrunner.

Six cartoon examples. Cartoons do visuals with obvious exaggeration, give insight into childlike fantasy, and come with large doses of exuberance and indignation.

> [A watermelon] smashed right on the top of his head and drove him into the earth up to the chin. (*Autobiography*)

> They tore half the clothes off me; they broke my arms and legs; they gave me a thump that dented the top of my head till it would hold coffee like a saucer; and . . . they threw me over the Niagara Falls, and I got wet. ("A Day at Niagara")

> A friend drops in to swap compliments with you, and freckles me with bullet-holes till my skin won't hold my principles. ("Journalism in Tennessee")

> [The effect of the burglar alarm] is to hurl you across the house and slam you against the wall and then curl you up and squirm you like a spider on a stove lid. ("The McWilliamses and the Burglar Alarm")

> [The boy sits on a powder keg when the alderman hits him] a whack in the rear with the flat of his hand; and in an instant that good little boy shot out through the roof and soared away toward the sun, with the fragments of those fifteen dogs stringing after him like the tail of a kite. ("The Story of the Good Little Boy")

> [The cat sleeps in a dynamite hole as the blast goes off.]
> In 'bout a minute we seen a puff of smoke bust up out of the hole, 'n' then everything let go with an awful crash, 'n' about four million ton of rocks 'n' dirt 'n' smoke 'n' splinters shot up 'bout a mile an' a half into the air, an' by George, right in the dead center of it was old Tom Quartz a goin' end over end, an' a snortin' an' a sneez'n, an' a clawin' an' a reachin' for things like all possessed. (*Roughing It*, Chapter 61)

Analysts, having pointed out Twain's uses of humor to prick the bubbles of human pomposity, to reveal ourselves as we truly are, and to open gaps in the garments of conformity, have seemed to focus on his indebtedness to the traditions of Southwestern humor, to the local colorists, and to the literary comedian. Other analysts have listed almost a score of stylistic devices used by nineteenth-century humorists and have cited Twain as the pre-eminent practitioner.

No doubt Twain can pass the cataloging test, and he can do it with most of the books he wrote, but what really makes him funny? It was chiefly, I believe, his posture and the piling-on and bubbling-along effect of his language. Just that—and it was enough to make him a unique comic force in America.

The Secret to Mark Twain's Performing Success

Marlene Boyd Vallin

Mark Twain's rapid rise from regional celebrity journalist to internationally known writer and American cultural icon were due in large part to his critically acclaimed national lecture tours, and he would continue to pursue this lucrative secondary career for more than four decades. In the following essay, Marlene Boyd Vallin suggests that Twain did not adhere to the conventional lecturing techniques of the day, which held no place for audience participation or feedback. Effective communication was central to Mark Twain's platform performances, Vallin suggests, and he achieved a unique atmosphere of intimacy with his audience by allowing their reaction to dictate his timing, content, and other aspects of his performance. Twain also effectively employed the element of surprise as a means of creating suspense, and sought throughout his career to perfect this and numerous other lecturing techniques. Vallin suggests that Twain's performance theories demonstrated an understanding of human behavior that anticipated the works of twentieth-century behavior psychologists and speech communication theorists. Marlene Boyd Vallin is an assistant professor of speech communication at the Pennsylvania State University, Berks Campus.

For more than forty years the renowned American author Mark Twain gained fame and fortune, nationally and internationally, as a platform performer. Shortly after his very successful first public engagement, "The Sandwich Island Lecture," delivered in San Francisco on October 2, 1866, his

Reprinted, with permission from the Bowling Green State University Popular Press, from "'Manner Is Everything': The Secret to Mark Twain's Performance Success," by Marlene Boyd Vallin, *Journal of Popular Culture*, vol. 23, no. 2 (Fall 1990), pp. 81–89. Endnotes in the original have been omitted in this reprint.

popularity as a speaker rose rapidly. Within three years, as a member of James Redpath's Boston Lyceum Bureau, he was advertised as America's favorite humorist. From November 1884 to February 1885, he, in partnership with the noted author George Washington Cable, performed over a hundred times in about eighty different cities in what was regarded as the most celebrated reading tour of the decade. Ten years later, accompanied by his wife and daughters, Twain embarked on a world tour beginning in Cleveland, Ohio, in July 1895, journeying westward to such locations as Canada, Australia and India, and culminating in London, England, in May 1896. Between and after these tours, Mark Twain was a much-in-demand occasional and after-dinner speaker, persistently perfecting this art before public and private audiences, for payment and gratis.

The people's desire to experience the captivating effects of communication with Samuel Langhorne Clemens's public persona, Mark Twain, seemed insatiable. His platform career transformed this creative genius from a regional journalist-lecturer whose appeal to audiences lay in the recreating of the character of the American West of the 1860s to that of a cultivated personality who appealed to many levels of society, including the most cultured, at home and abroad. Indeed, the highly favorable response from his first public lecture, a decision he made based more on the need for money than the desire to talk, became the turning point of his life. It was this "alternate career," as he later called his platform performing, that not only sustained him financially, but also, more importantly, was instrumental in the development of Mark Twain, the celebrated personality and consummate communicator.

SOURCES

In spite of the conclusion that it was Twain's platform career that contributed much to the development of his great talent, relatively little has been written about this profound influence. The few books, journal articles, and theses available tend to chronicle his performance; none examines them as examples of effective communication.

The material available for a study of Twain's platform talent is all of a secondary nature. A phonograph recording was made of his "Seventieth Birthday Speech," but it was ruined. Fortunately, however, Twain did make comments on his perceptions of the speaking process in his notebooks, autobiography, and letters. Other sources of information about his delivery must be gleaned from the comments of contemporaries in newspapers and magazines, and from recollections in biographical accounts. Copies of some of the texts of Twain's programs were printed in local newspapers, but their reliability, as to reflecting what was actually said, is questionable for several reasons. On discovering such a publication, Twain often reacted angrily by altering the lecture or discarding it altogether. He contended that such prior knowledge would dampen the appeal

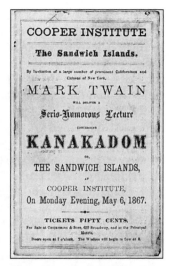

This sign advertises Twain's lecture at the Cooper Institute in New York.

of the lecture for the next audience. What Twain planned to say and what occurred on the occasion did not often agree. Although he advocated memorization over recitation as the preferred method for speaking in public, he often experienced lapses in memory. Interestingly, his spontaneous reactions to these lapses were found to bring forth some of his more favorable responses from audiences. As Twain became more experienced and more popular, he dispensed with memorizing a manuscript. Instead, he chose to prepare his performances based on a page of symbols which represented the scope of his talk. With such notations at the podium, all he needed to do was glance at the pictures to prompt his recollection. Freedom from a verbatim script enabled him to do what he thought best for the success of his performance—to relate extemporaneously to his audience. To discover why Twain was such a popular platform performer, it is necessary for the researcher to reconstruct his performances depending on notations made by Twain and his contemporaries. Needless to say, no collection of words can impart what actually occurred when Twain interacted with his public.

The purpose of this essay is to establish that Mark Twain's success on the platform was the result of his fascination with the communication process. From years of observation and experience, he developed insights about public platform speaking which might be called a theory of performance. The discussion will focus on the question: What was it about Twain's oral presentations which made him so popular? He once said: "I know a great many secrets about audiences— secrets not to be gotten out of books, but acquired only by experience." What were these secrets, how did he learn them, and how did he use this knowledge to prepare and present his platform presentations? These secrets became the bases for his performance theory. Specifically, this paper will present and discuss Twain's performance theory by establishing what it was, how it evolved, and how it was manifested in his public lectures.

DELIVERY

The secrets about audiences which Twain claimed to know, which formed his theory of performance, came from the source of all his learning—the do-it-yourself school of watching and trying. Occasions for speech were commonplace in nineteenth-century America. Circuits of public speaking sponsored by lyceums and, later, Chautauquas abounded. Inhabitants of the smallest towns witnessed public speaking by preachers, politicians, and players. Like Twain, the constituents of this dynamic, developing society were especially fascinated with all things American, especially the sound of the language. Talk tended to be the national pastime. Therefore, it is justifiable to infer that young Samuel Clemens of Hannibal, Missouri, must have been quite familiar with the process of oral presentation at an early age.

However, not until 1867, while listening to a sermon in a Universalist church in Brooklyn, did Twain realize his most important secret about audiences. Watching intensely as the Reverend Dr. Chapin held his audience spellbound, Twain observed that there seemed to be an invisible connection between the listener's soul and the preacher's head, along which traveled in ceaseless flow the living spirit of words. Never before had he seen such rapt attention in an audience. Twain reasoned that it was not *what* Chapin said that made him so powerful, it was *how* he said it. "Manner is everything," he concluded. This truth, something he had sensed but could not specify previously, became the basis for his performance theory. Henceforth, he consciously contrived his presentations with delivery as the most important consideration. In order to achieve success with an audience—that is, to fulfill one's purpose for performing, all efforts must be focused on delivery. With the perfection of delivery devices, the lines of communication are installed between speaker and listener, providing for the vital exchange of meaning.

Acknowledging the importance of delivery as the chief means for maintaining the attention of audiences was nothing new, especially in nineteenth-century America. During the nineteenth century, every professional speaker was concerned with that canon of classical rhetoric referred to as delivery. The prescribed method for learning about platform techniques was to study with an elocutionist. Most elocutionists . . . professed that specific study in voice and bodily action was necessary in order to be [an] effective speaker. Delivery was stressed as an end in itself. Therefore, in Twain's time, most of the speakers that American audiences were exposed to were practitioners of these contrived vocal and body gymnastics. Accordingly, the public expected to play the part of passive observers to such dramatic display.

In contrast, Twain's thoughts on delivery reflect the thinking of one ahead of his time. While the focus of elocution-trained speakers was on how they were sounding and appearing, Twain's concentration was on how his audience was responding. To Twain, perfecting delivery was not an end in itself as it became for many of the elocutionists; on the contrary, delivery was the most crucial means for achieving what he believed to be the purpose of oral presentations—to create a desired effect on his auditors. In other words, the theories of communication effectiveness, based on the findings of behavior psychologists and formulated in the twentieth century by such scholars as James Winans and Charles Woolbert, were anticipated by Twain a half century earlier. Although self-taught, Twain was a keen observer of people's actions. As his friend William Dean Howells exclaimed, "He knew all the stops in that simple instrument, man." Twain understood speaking in public to be a transactional process with meaning located in the perceptions of the listeners, not only in the speaker's intent. Speakers must be aware of audience response; they must prepare their programs with this in mind. Since Twain's obvious purpose as a performer was to entertain, audience feedback in the form of uproarious laughter signaled his success. Achieving unity with his audience was what kept Twain coming back to the platform for forty years.

Perceiving oral presentations as communicative acts, Twain realized another "secret" about audiences—that the speaker must adjust his discourse to relate directly to them—their needs, their experiences, and their ability to relate to the speaker. In other words, Twain's rhetoric was that of identification. His use of a chatty, conversational speaking style devoid of facial and bodily expression, his dependence on self-deprecating humor along with his personification of characters of questionable reputation, and his apparently shy, unpolished demeanor soon endeared him to audiences. Americans were tiring of the pretentious, pompous style advocated by the dominant Victorian culture; they grew to prefer Twain's performing style of naturalness, individuality, and authenticity. His was a popular appeal. In an age sur-

---

MARK TWAIN'S PASSION FOR LECTURING

Paul Fatout is the author of Mark Twain on the Lecture Circuit. *In the following excerpt, he notes that, despite Twain's best efforts, he was never able to swear off lecturing for long.*

Whatever the wellspring of his desire to stand and deliver before an audience, Mark Twain was a stupendous talker, who never lost his fondness for the platform. Yet to hear him tell it, he found public speaking unrewarding, detestable, infamous drudgery. Repeatedly airing his hatred of the onerous business, he raged about the hardships of lecture tours, missed connections, tiresome train rides, nondescript small towns, barren hotels and their rascally proprietors, cranky audiences, bores, obnoxious committee men, and a multitude of irritations that touched off his explosive emotions. Nevertheless, despite violent complaints, swearing off over and over, and permanently retiring just as often, the lure was irresistible. When he was almost fifty he said to an interviewer: "I love the platform, and I would like to live on it but I cannot be traveling about all the time." Five months before his death he confessed to a correspondent that after a successful lecturing career he had expected to savor the freedom of release from its exhausting demands, but that he had not enjoyed the freedom. We may surmise that only poor health prevented him from responding to the urge to the last day.

Paul Fatout, *Mark Twain on the Lecture Circuit.* Bloomington: Indiana University Press, 1960.

feited with elocutionists and rules of propriety, Twain's apparent lack of art was his greatest allure. He also posed, but his was the posture of an inept, unsure amateur, and both he and his audiences mutually recognized this behavior as a humorous device. Growing up in a Southern slave state, learning his craft in the wild West, and settling in the traditional East, Twain symbolized the quintessential American for his audiences; he related well to them.

On the surface, Twain's purpose for lecturing seemed to be to entertain, but a closer look at his messages reveals that his real goal was to instruct. Twain used humor as a means to achieve this end: "Humor must not professedly teach, it must not professedly preach, but it must do both if it would live forever." Recognition of the universal appeal of humor demonstrates that Twain knew another "secret" about his audiences. His audiences liked to laugh, and more importantly, they needed to laugh. Setting his humor in pathos, Twain aimed for the feeling level in his listeners. He made them feel good—something many inhabitants in dreary towns truly needed. He appealed to the common folk with his common-sense messages replete with comical anecdotes and horse sense. Camouflaging his moral messages in the cloak of comedy, he succeeded in achieving his objective. A generous dose of native humor coupled with simple, truth-revealing logic proved very appealing to the average nineteenth-century American.

THE ELEMENT OF SURPRISE

Another "secret" which Twain knew about audiences and which he used expertly was that people tend to be attentive when the element of surprise is used. Knowing what will come defuses the excitement of the occasion; keeping listeners in suspense heightens the mood of the event and encourages greater audience participation. In other words, anticipation breeds active participation which leads to greater communication effectiveness. Twain fashioned his total performance with this "secret" in mind—from preparing the public for his appearance, to his introduction to the platform, throughout the preparation of his lecture, to his exit. For example, he would often stimulate interest in his program by planting advertisements and letters to the editor in local newspapers warning that "The trouble begins at eight" or detailing what not to expect. He would also have handbills distributed which announced the lecture and the time and place, followed by exaggerated false details of the event. These preliminaries were designed to tease the public into attending. Instead of allowing himself to be introduced by another in the usual way, which he detested, he preferred to stumble onto the stage, stare embarrassingly at the audience, deceive them into thinking that he was the introducer, and then, eventually, introduce himself. Other times, he planned his introduction so that when the curtain opened he would be playing the piano—again appearing totally unprepared for the occasion. The purpose of these "starters," as he called these devices, was to "warm-up" his audiences for his lectures. When he was ready to present his talk, he would often begin in the conventional way—book or manuscript in hand, and then he would use what he called "this new dodge." Pausing to make some apparently impromptu explanatory comments, he would, instead of returning to his script, continue the rest of his program in that same manner—chatting about events and stories and going off on carefully planned tangents *just* at the most important points. Before the audience realized it, the lecture was over, and the listeners were left laughing heartily in delightful surprise. With this method Twain claimed, "You'll never lose your audience—not even for a moment." The element of surprise was also worked into Twain's exits. Maintaining the effect of apparent unpreparedness, he feigned confusion over the direction off the stage, oftentimes using the wrong door. Needless to say, . . . the audience was left laughing in their seats. Twain's meticulously planned strategy of surprise, including his reliance on what contemporary comedians call "shtick," contributed to his obtaining the total involvement of the audience.

Although Twain's platform performances are listed under lecture tours and reading tours, they generally followed the same format—extemporaneous renderings of his written works, set in a lecture based on autobiographical experiences. "The persona of the story seemed generally crucial in his selections." He became the embodiment of these characterizations within his own works, for he believed that the actor contributed more than half of the meaning of a creation. His friend Howells agreed: "What we have strongly conceived we ought to make others strongly imagine, and we ought to use every genuine art to that end." Above all, the parts of his written work which were most successful with his audiences, were those materials which reflected a humorous, yet commonsense, vernacular perspective. Twain used material from a variety of his writings: *The Prince and the Pauper, The Adventures of Huckleberry Finn, Roughing It, Innocents Abroad, Pudd'nhead Wilson.* In later years his repertoire generally consisted of stories from his three principal lectures: "The Sandwich Islands," "The American Vandal Abroad," and "Roughing It." Twain considered "The Celebrated Jumping Frog of Calaveras County" as his most successful story: "Nothing in this world can best *that* yarn when one is feeling good and has the right audience in front of him." In summary, Twain selected material that tended to be somewhat autobiographical, with characterization as its central feature, containing content with popular appeal.

REHEARSED SPONTANEITY

Twain regarded preparation as "[his] duty to [his] audience." Through practice and observation he carefully honed his apparently artless art. He learned that audiences respond more favorably to spontaneity, so he adapted his written material to effect what Winans was to later call "a lively sense of communication." That is, he recognized that there are differences between the processes of writing and speaking: "Print is the proper vehicle for written speech, but the moment 'talk' is put into print you recognize that it is not what [it] was when you read it; you perceive that an immense something has disappeared from it. That's its soul." Therefore, "written things . . . have to be limbered up, broken up, colloquialized, and turned into common forms of unpremeditated talk—otherwise they will bore the house, not entertain it." To Twain, there was nothing more appealing than "the captivating naturalness of an impromptu narration."

Working at maintaining that enchanting element of surprise, Twain meticulously rehearsed pauses into his works. That "impressive silence, that eloquent silence, that geometrically progressive silence which often achieves a desired effect where no combination of words howsoever felicitous could accomplish it" he regarded as the most effective device of delivery. He was most concerned about the timing of the pause, and carefully watched the facial expressions of the listeners to determine the right moment to bring it to an end. Twain explained, "If the pause is too short the impressive point is passed, and the audience has had time to divine that a surprise is intended—and you can't surprise them, of course." According to one observer, "Twain knew how to make one second of silence outweigh a hundred words."

Since Twain wished to achieve an air of spontaneity in his performances, he prepared the reading of his narratives to be delivered without the book. Reading from the book, he explained, "renders the nicest shadings of delivery impossible. I mean those studied fictions which seem to be the impulse of the moment and which are so effective: such as, for instance, fictitious hesitancies for the right word, fictitious unconscious pauses, fictitious unconscious side remarks, fictitious unconscious embarrassment, fictitious unconscious emphases placed upon the wrong word with a deep intention back of it." With a book, "the reader is telling another person's tale at secondhand; you are a mimic and not the person involved; you are artificiality, not a reality." The reader from a book does not get at the "heart" of the audience.

In preparing for his earlier performances, Twain tried to memorize passages with a unique system of mnemonics. However, since he learned that audiences differ and that his effectiveness depended upon the listeners' responses, he eventually prepared his material in notes so as to adjust his message accordingly. Above all, Twain advocated much rehearsal so that the speaker's delivery was "limbered up so that it will seem impromptu to an audience."

The lines of communication between speaker and listener must be established early and maintained throughout the presentation. All of the performer's efforts, according to Twain, must be focused on that fascinating interaction. Concentrating on delivery as the chief channel to effect the speaker's purpose, Mark Twain became one of the most captivating speakers of his time. For many, he had no equal. Compared with the popular contemporary, humorist Artemus Ward, Twain was "a mammoth circus chandelier" and Ward "a penn'orth of tallow."

Perhaps the best description of his physical appearance as well as his delivery style comes from this article appearing in a late-nineteenth-century issue of *The Critic* magazine:

> [F]or the most part, he talks in low, slow, conversational tones, at times he rises to real burst of eloquence—not the polished grandiloquent eloquence of the average American speaker, but the eloquence conveyed in simple words and phrases, and promoted by some deep and sincerely felt sentiment.

Mark Twain steals unobtrusively on to the platform, dressed in the regulation evening-clothes, with the trouser-pockets cut high up, into which he occasionally drives both hands. He bows with a quiet dignity to the roaring cheers which greet him at every "At Home." Then, with natural, unaffected gesture, and with scarcely any prelude, he gets under way with his first story. He is a picturesque figure on the stage. His long, shaggy, white hair surmounts a face full of intellectual fire. The eyes, arched with bushy brows, and which seem to be closed most of the time while he is speaking, flash out now and then from their deep sockets with a genial, kindly, pathetic look, and the face is deeply drawn with furrows accumulated during an existence of sixty years. He talks in short sentences, with a peculiar smack of the lips at the end of each. His language is just that of his books, full of the quaintest Americanisms. . . . His figure is rather slight, not above middle height, and the whole man suggests an utter lack of physical energy . . . Mark Twain stands perfectly still in one place during the whole of the time he is talking to the audience. He rarely moves his arms, unless it is to adjust his spectacles or to show by action how a certain thing was done. His characteristic attitude is to stand quite still, with the right arm across the abdomen and the left resting on it and supporting his chin. In this way he talks on for nearly two hours; and, while the audience is laughing uproariously, he never by any chance relapses into a smile.

To have read Mark Twain is a delight. But to have seen and heard him is a joy not readily to be forgotten.

HIS ARTLESS ART

Indeed, attempts to capture the charismatic performances of Mark Twain on paper are impossible, as many reporters of his time openly confessed. Comments have been made on his slow speech, his exaggerated drawl that came and went at will, the slightly nasal quality, his sometimes too soft voice that would unexpectedly burst into eloquence, and the precision with which he used the pause. Many have marveled at his mastery of the vernacular in language as well as in characterizations, his talent for recreating those memorable characters with a wink of an eye, and his fixed focus on having fun. Others were struck by his semicomatose stance and that unflappable deadpan expression. And all were awed by his startling appearance, that shock of white hair and those eagle-like eyes. His apparently artless art was most demanding, and he never ceased perfecting it. According to his friend Howells, "He was the most consummate performer I ever saw."

Despite the difficult lifestyle of the tour—one-night stands, hard travel, and loneliness—Twain loved the platform. Scholars who have written about his "alternate career" tend to agree that he needed it, for the development of his personality and of his art. Certainly, his audiences needed him. Twain's performing technique shows an uncommon fascination with the social transaction that happens when one confronts an audience. His genius seemed to lay in his perception of the speaking situation as an intimate relationship and in his relentless drive to refine the bond. His sensitivity for the human spirit set him out above the rest. "People can always talk well when they are talking what they feel," he wrote; "this is the secret of eloquence." Yes, Mark Twain knew a great many secrets about audiences. These secrets became the basis for what might be called his performance theory—insights which presaged modern communication theory.

Mark Twain: Professional Traveler

Gary Charles Smith

Gary Charles Smith argues that Samuel Clemens's compulsion to travel was synonymous with his yearning for truth and deeper understanding of human nature, and that traveling afforded him the opportunity to observe people from all walks of life and social classes. Smith notes that Clemens's wanderlust led him across the Atlantic Ocean no less than twenty-seven times during his lifetime. Clemens also explored Europe, Asia, the South Pacific, and the Middle-East, to say nothing of Canada and the United States. The fruits of these travels would heavily influence the stories produced by Clemens's writing persona, Mark Twain. As Smith points out, Twain's early novels began as travel diaries, and virtually all of Clemens's many journeys would find their way into his fiction eventually. Smith is a professor at North Carolina State University.

To a large degree, Mark Twain's prolific literary efforts grew out of his many journeys at home and abroad. In his travels, he witnessed and later wrote about practically all he had experienced. From his first short trips as apprentice printer to his longer voyages as a professional traveler, he saw it all: violence, humor, crime, and at times, love. Widely cosmopolitan in his interests, in his experience of life, and in the sources and influences which helped to develop his talents as a writer, Mark Twain revealed his America satirically but truthfully. His memorable characters, places, and events all stem from his journey through life; his literary genius gave them immortality.

In his *Autobiography,* Mark Twain, after witnessing a young boy stabbed to death by a drunken man, said, "I saw

Excerpted from "The Influence of Mark Twain's Journeys on His Work," by Gary Charles Smith, *Mark Twain Journal*, vol. 20, no. 1 (Winter 1979–1980), pp. 10–14. Reprinted with permission. Endnotes in the original have been omitted in this reprint.

the red life gush from his breast." The remark underscored not only Twain's closeness to life's realities, but also his feelings for his fellow man. Few American writers in the nineteenth century traveled as much as Twain, and, as a consequence, his travels became his fiction. Like the river pilot, Twain ". . . reads nature unobstructed by stereotyped responses to scenery." He did not attempt psychological escape; rather, he found that travel follows the great circle back to self. In his own ego is the story of all successes and defeats; his work is a result of his intense need to see, to know, and most certainly, to understand.

MANY WELL-DOCUMENTED JOURNEYS

His compulsion to travel, as well as his obsession to note everything he saw, took him on thirty-four long journeys. He crossed the Atlantic no fewer than twenty-seven times. He saw the Orient, Hawaii, and of course, "his" America. Once, when he was questioned about his compulsive travels by a reporter for the *New York World*, he replied, "There always was an imperative reason. I had to gather materials for my books." The "materials" came from Twain's experiences as a printer, river pilot, miner, reporter, lecturer and traveler par excellence.

His "books" include travel books, three of foreign travel: *Innocents Abroad, A Tramp Abroad*, and *Following the Equator*, and two books on America: *Roughing It* and *Life on the Mississippi*. Actually, he was writing fiction before, during, and after the sojourns; however, most of what we read in his novels and short stories are literary by-products of his own experiences. For instance, in the Preface to *The Adventures of Tom Sawyer*, Twain declares, "Most of the adventures in this book really occurred; one or two were experiences of my own. The rest were those of boys who were schoolmates of mine." Twain told the story in the third person realizing that Tom was an unlikely subject for satire. However, the novel introduced Huck Finn, whom Twain allowed, out of necessity, to tell his own story in *The Adventures of Huckleberry Finn*. Importantly, while this novel was being pieced together by Twain, the author took time to travel to Bermuda, Canada and Europe and to publish *A Tramp Abroad, The Prince and the Pauper*, and *Life on the Mississippi*. Obviously, his mind was constantly at work, recording fact and later transferring fact into imagination.

Whether or not *Huck Finn* was the better or worse for Twain's breaking off his writing to travel belongs on the critics' table. But at least one critic, Charles Neider, suggests that Twain's revisiting Hannibal, which he recounts in *Life on the Mississippi*, inspired the completion of *Huck Finn.*

By 1867, Twain had survived his father's death, an eventful boyhood (to say the least) in Florida and Hannibal, Missouri, had traveled to Iowa, Nevada, St. Louis, Philadelphia, New York, San Francisco, Hawaii, passed through the Isthmus to New York again, worked as a printer, miner, acquired a river pilot's license, served briefly with a company of Confederate volunteers (who would later serve as models for Tom Sawyer's gang), had written articles for various newspapers, published *The Celebrated Jumping Frog of Calaveras County and Other Sketches,* and had relinquished the name of Samuel L. Clemens for Mark Twain. The experience of these journeys, occupations, and the "education" Twain received during these years were called upon in his later literary work. He would soon find himself a teacher, but never a lover, of all. He had, like Huck, seen too much too soon.

MARK TWAIN'S FIRST TRAVELS ABROAD

His first trip around the world, which resulted in *Innocents Abroad,* began in June, 1867; the account was published in book form in 1869. Twain's "Innocents" were the American tourists whom he joined on the ship "Quaker City" which left New York bound east for Europe and the Holy Land. Twain's idea was to travel and write letters about his experiences. Ironically, this westerner traveling out of New York created a controversy between East and West. The California *ALTA* [newspaper], which had financed his trip with the right to publish his colorful letters, was at odds with a Hartford publisher, Elisha Bliss, who proposed to bring out the letters in a travel book. This incident will serve as an example of Twain's unfortunate financial concerns that plagued him throughout his life. Such "misunderstandings" appear and reappear in Twain's fiction. His characters are often caught in the middle. The dilemma of "nigger" Jim, who might either be "saved" by Huck and Tom's romantic antics or be sent home to slavery, in *Huck Finn* is typical Twain lore.

Innocents Abroad was originally entitled, and eventually subtitled, *The New Pilgrim's Progress.* Twain's American tourists, like [Henry] James's American who said, "I know nothing about history, or art, or foreign tongues, or any other learned matters," must travel to find understanding. In spite of Twain's superficial coverings of laughter and comedy, however, there seems to be a tragic, darker world beneath the surface; no trip is without some recognition of evil at work in the world. The ship that carried Twain and his fellow voyagers is a microcosm of humanity. The "innocents" are likened to the tribes of Israel in search of the Promised Land. As Twain, and America would have it, however, the Pilgrims arrived back in America happy the voyage was over. One cannot help but think of Huck Finn's famous remark at the end of his "voyage" of enlightenment in the concerns of the real world, "But I reckon I got to light out for the territory ahead of the rest, because Aunt Sally she is going to adopt me and sivilize me and I can't stand it. I been there before." . . .

Twain's book recalling his earlier travels in the American west, *Roughing It*, published in 1872, traces, as one critic states, ". . . his experience of the journey. There is no doubt of the exhilaration, the excitement, the thrill of it." However, Professor Martin, in his chapter on Twain in *Harvests of Change*, maintains that the work represents more of Twain's imagination at work than it does his memory of the events. Twain, viewing Europe and the eastern United States as mostly corrupt, tried to recapture the openness and splendor of the exciting West as he had seen it when he was sixteen. For this trip, he needed only two "innocents": himself and his brother Orion. The book is filled with anecdotes and tall stories, some of which perhaps were "reheated" to serve for the "true stories" that are heard by such as Tom and Huck on and off the river. *Roughing It* is the initiation of the tenderfoot to the American West. Here, as he had done in *Innocents Abroad*, and he will do in *Life on the Mississippi*, Twain utilized his technique of incorporating daily humorous anecdotes into a larger narrative.

Following the writing of *The Gilded Age* (1873) in collaboration with Charles Dudley Warner, Twain embarked on his second trip to England during which time the germ of *The Prince and the Pauper* and *A Connecticut Yankee in King Arthur's Court* was being conceived. In 1876, probably recalling his old times on the Mississippi, Twain wrote and published *Tom Sawyer.* Actually, he had begun the novel as early as 1870 but, as he says, the "tank" ran dry and he had to wait a few years before finishing it. He acquired the flood of recollections from his boyhood in Hannibal from the articles Howells had requested him to write for *The Atlantic.*

As a result of travels in Germany and Italy in 1878–79, Twain published *A Tramp Abroad* (1880), the literary offspring of his walking tour with his life-long friend [Joseph] Twitchell. Aside from having some fun with the German language (in *Life on the Mississippi* Twain tells us he mastered the "language" of the river) in the work, Twain again used the opportunity of his journey to criticize the old masters of Europe.

A Tramp Abroad was followed by *The Prince and the Pauper* (1882) and by *Life on the Mississippi* (1883). Although separated in time and place, these two works manifest some of Twain's traditional literary lore. The pauper, Tom Canby, strongly suggests an amalgam of the characteristics of Huck Finn and Tom Sawyer. The disguise motif is utilized in both books: Tom's masquerading as the prince in the former and, the ostensible Ohio farmer who is, in reality, a sophisticated river gambler, will serve as an example in the latter. Twain, encountering frauds and imposters everywhere he traveled, later makes fictional characters out of them. In these two works his technique is to place his contemporaries in a previous time in history: sixteenth-century England for *The Prince and the Pauper*, and the 1850's in America and the Mississippi in *Life on the Mississippi*. Indeed, Twain owed as much to his travels in Europe as he did to his early experiences on the Mississippi. While composing *The Prince and the Pauper*, Twain never forgot to utilize his memories of his own youth in Hannibal, nor in the writing of *Life on the Mississippi* could he forget England's ironic gift to the American South: [Sir Walter] Scott's romantic novels and their questionable influence on a part of Twain's America.

IN SEARCH OF TRUTH

In 1885 *The Adventures of Huckleberry Finn* was finally completed for publication. Going back once again to Tom Sawyer's Hannibal, Twain revived Huck Finn and developed him into one of the most meaningful characters in fiction. [Literary critic] Alexander Cowie notes "Many of the 'Gothic' elements in Mark Twain's stories about boyhood were not derived from books but were transferred from the tongues of real boys of Hannibal—of whom Sam Clemens was one." Although *Tom Sawyer* is much the better unified novel when compared with *Huck Finn,* the latter reflects a serious vision of Twain's sentiment toward man. A comprehensive study of the world of the Mississippi, it serves as a microcosm for Mark Twain's America. Twain's usual humor and delight often mask its tragic meaning. Unlike Tom Sawyer, Twain's young spokesman is not easily fooled by illusions.

There is a striking similarity between Huck and Twain. Huck's early formal training or lack of it is akin to that of Twain's. Both learn from their journeys that what seems to be is not always what is. [Literary critic] Ludwig Lewisohn calls Twain "The average adolescent-minded American-rooter at ballgames, political banquets, exhibitions of pseudo-heroic claptrap. He was that man plus genius. He was Huck Finn grown up." Then the critic adds that these things make Twain unique and precious. Many critics have sensed Twain's dual personality, manifested in the fictive natures of Tom Sawyer and Huck Finn. But one thing is evident: he was not divided from his own kind of people—the Tom Sawyers, the Huck Finns and the Hank Morgans of America. If their characters are divided, it is, as [literary critic] Carl Van Doren states, not in their intrinsic make up, but in what the United States failed to make them.

Huck refuses to endure a false dilemma; there has to be, for him and for Twain, another place, another way out. For instance, in *The Adventures of Huckleberry Finn,* Huck, after being repeatedly told how to behave and warned of his punishment by Miss Watson, reflects, "She told me all about the bad place and I said I wished I was there. All I wanted was to go somewhere else; all I wanted was a change." The statement in effects masks the author's compulsion to travel, to learn the truth, if there were any truth to be known. Twain's fiction infers that the world is made up of much the same types of people Huck encountered on his trip down the Mississippi; the reader is left to his own conclusions. The book could be retitled "Huck's Life on the Mississippi"; it is so close to Twain's earlier voyages in 1857 and 1883. Twain learned early that every journey toward a new birth had to be preceded by the death of a previous one. The partly optimistic Mark Twain of *Roughing It* is antithetical to the pessimistic Mark Twain of *The Mysterious Stranger,* in the same way the Huck Finn who lives with Widow Douglas in the beginning of the novel is greatly changed to the Huck who has had his fill of civilization.

Twain's next novel *A Connecticut Yankee in King Arthur's Court* (1889), was written between his lecture tour with George Washington Cable and his latest trip to Europe 1891–93. Anecdotes from his previous voyages to England, thoughts about *The Prince and the Pauper*, his own interests in gadgets, new printing processes, his life-long disdain for authority and his concern with the robber barons in America all went into the composition of this novel. Twain's hero is Hank Morgan, an American, born and reared in Hartford, Connecticut. He freely tells us "So I am a Yankee of the Yankees—and practical." A self-made supervisor in an arms factory, he is transported back to the sixth century to Arthur's Camelot. In telling the tale, Twain used his familiar technique of having his speaker meet someone while on a journey who has written the account. Then Twain proceeds to read us the stranger's story. Again Twain's "stranger" is the author himself, disguising himself to launch us into a satire of the past. . . .

In both *The Prince and the Pauper* and *A Connecticut Yankee in King Arthur's Court* Twain revisits the same theme as a prince and a king masquerade among their subjects as commoners, viewing the hidden depths of life. Their journeys are their enlightenment, but Twain cannot have them see as clearly as he sees. One can only speculate whether or not either of them learned anything. Twain's view is purposely not an optimistic one. The voyage, however, must be made if ignorance and intolerance are to be exposed. . . .

The Tragedy of Pudd'nhead Wilson was Twain's last novel that takes the reader back to Twain's life on the Mississippi. 1895–96 saw the author on a different kind of journey, a world lecture tour to pay off his debts. When the Paige Typesetter and the Webster Publishing Company had both failed, Twain, like Sir Walter Scott, refused to take advantage of the bankruptcy laws and assumed his debt. But as he lifted himself from debt, another tragedy affected his life. His daughter Susy had died at home in Hartford. But the books continued to come forth: a refuge against despair. . . .

Following the Equator (1897) is Twain's last book of travel. [Historian] Bernard De Voto is correct in his assessment of the work. He sees it as the dullest of Twain's books, a task without heart, undertaken for money alone. In *Following the Equator* Twain has his persona retracing the trip he made years before. But this time he is searching for peace and ease, not adventure and lore for his creative talents. He has succeeded in adapting all of his life's journeys to his fiction. He is a man bound to an endless voyage to an unknown destination.

TRAVEL AS A STUDY IN HUMAN NATURE

Twain's works of fiction usually followed his frequent journeys. The travel books began as diaries which evolved, with the help of Twain's ability to perceive even the smallest detail clearly and his sardonic humor, into lasting pieces of American literature. *The Sketches* from Calaveras County recorded his experiences in the West. *Tom Sawyer, Huck Finn,* and *Pudd'nhead Wilson* traced his boyhood and his initiation into the adult world. *The Prince and the Pauper* and *A Connecticut Yankee in King Arthur's Court* revealed his political and social concerns and also brought out his interest in Europe and its past. And certainly "Hadleyburg" is Hannibal.

His travels put him in contact with men and women from all classes of society. His genius lies in his ability to see what we do not see. The London Museum, for instance, humbles most of us, but Twain sees more than appearances. One Saturday, while visiting the museum he remarked " . . . the British Museum is full of preachers stealing sermons for the next day!" To Twain, all men are similar regardless of nationalities. For example, a Frenchman is not simply a Frenchman in Twain's penetrating vision. He discerns much more: "The Frenchman is nothing if not pious . . . he requires his neighbor to be pious also—otherwise he will kill him and *make* him so." And so, *Joan of Arc* is conceived.

Mark Twain's purpose was to write realistically about what he experienced in his journey through life. To accomplish this end, he used whatever vantage point he believed would offer the best means; consequently, we are more "in" a fictive situation than we are outsiders, viewing the action. A large part of this involvement is due to Twain's ability to harmonize his style with the tone of what is happening. Whether or not we enter into Twain's world by way of a stagecoach, a riverboat, a raft, an ocean liner or a walking tour of Europe makes little difference. His insight into the human character is limitless, even if his hope is not. "Mainly, he told the truth."

Championing American Literature

Shelley Fisher Fishkin

Shelley Fisher Fishkin recounts an experience she had at a literature seminar in England, in which a British professor proclaimed his dislike of *The Adventures of Huckleberry Finn* and expressed bewilderment over the fact that Americans hold this novel in such high regard. She notes that negative responses from abroad to Twain's work are nothing new, and that they suggest Twain met his objective of creating fiction that was uniquely and unabashedly American in spirit, rather than an adherence to the British and European cultural sensibilities that had hitherto been considered as the standard for American literature. Twain's fiction flouted the excesses of ornateness and sentimentality in Victorian-era prose, and instead featured the regional dialect of frontier America—a dialect which he felt reflected the unpretentiousness, practicality and ingenuity of his countrymen. Furthermore, Fisher Fishkin notes, Twain's literature featured main characters previously deemed unworthy of such attention—uneducated children, slaves and servants—whose morality often far exceeded that of the "culturally refined" characters they encountered. Shelley Fisher Fishkin has a Ph.D. in American Studies, and is author of the award winning book *Was Huck Black: Mark Twain and African American Voices.*

February 1993. The chill mist that seemed to hang permanently over Cambridge, England, enveloped me as I headed toward the river from my apartment in Clare Hall, the postgraduate college at the University of Cambridge where I was a Visiting Fellow. Crossing Grange Road, I passed the King's

College School, where my youngest son was enrolled for the year. When told that his school was founded by Henry VI, he had been unimpressed: the dates of English history were just a blur to him at the time. But his eyes had opened wide when he was told that if you wanted to pass the geography course when the school was set up, you had to know that the world was flat. I crossed the river and entered the central court of a college founded more than five hundred years before the birth of the man I was scheduled to lecture on this evening.

The American Literature Seminar, sponsored by the university's English department, was a small monthly gathering of faculty and graduate students that met in Clare College. I arrived at the seminar room. Introductions were made. One person was working on Henry James, one on [Nathaniel] Hawthorne, one on T.S. Eliot, one on William Carlos Williams, and so on. Wine was passed around. The atmosphere was convivial as we took our seats at a large round table and I summarized my research on the influence of African-American voices on *Adventures of Huckleberry Finn*. I spoke for an hour and a lively discussion followed for another hour.

Then a silver-haired don who had been completely silent all evening suddenly exploded. "This is going to sound very negative, but I can't figure out what you Americans *see* in this book," he sputtered. "Don't you know it's a *bad* book?"

I could hardly suppress a smile. For Twain had set out to write a book that broke all the rules of English-novel-writing, and the don's outburst was clear testimony to the fact that he had succeeded in doing just that.

"Some Americans actually agree with your appraisal of the novel," I replied. I cited [author] Julius Lester's dismissal of the book as "a fantasy of adolescence," a "dismal portrait of the white male psyche," a bad book in which freedom means simply "freedom from restraint and responsibility." The don looked pleased.

"But," I continued, "you're right that most of us don't share your views." (When I had read Lester's comments aloud to [American author] Ralph Ellison in 1991, Ellison was aghast: "Oh my God. Where did he write that? . . . My God—how can he say that it was an irresponsible idea of freedom?") "Twain wanted to do something that hadn't been tried before," I continued. "He wanted to write a book no Englishman could even conceive of at the time—a book written in the voice of a child who skipped school and never learned proper grammar, who was not ashamed of his ignorance and who was convinced—quite rightly—that we would care about what he had to say nonetheless. Everything changed on the literary landscape after this book appeared: it made [Ernest] Hemingway, [William] Faulkner, Ellison—twentieth-century American fiction—*possible*." At this point the graduate students jumped in, and before the evening was over Twain had clearly come out on top.

When the seminar ended, I made my way out of the college gates, turning back for a moment for a last look at the perfectly proportioned, palatial Clare College courtyard. What an appropriate setting, I thought, in which to defend the book which served as America's literary declaration of independence. For Clare had been the college of Charles Townsend, Chancellor of the Exchequer, who had been responsible for imposing the taxes which precipitated what the English call the "American War of Independence." And Clare had also been the college of Lord Cornwallis, who had surrendered his army to the American troops, at Yorktown in 1781. America, young as she is, seems to have had a fairly long history of flummoxing Clare men.

Outside the United States, in other former European colonies, *Huckleberry Finn* is often taught as a model of how one breaks free from the colonizer's culture to create an indigenous national literature. Maria Alejandra Rosarossa, a professor in Buenos Aires, claims Twain as an "American" writer in the hemispheric sense of the word for precisely this reason—his ability to illuminate "a problematic issue" shared by every culture in North and South America: "its colonial origin." She believes he is valued in Argentina in part for his adeptness at showing "the tension between the unauthorized culture, the periphery, the border, and the authorized central one, continuously in conflict, both in the States and in Latin America." Similarly, political scientist Ralph Buultjens recalls that when he was a schoolboy in Sri Lanka, *Huckleberry Finn* was presented as an example of how you create literature in English that has next to nothing to do with England.

STARTING SOMETHING NEW

The irate Cambridge don would have agreed, most likely, with the British publication that in 1870 found Twain to be "a very offensive specimen of the vulgarest kind of Yankee." This is not to say that all British readers denied Twain respect. On the contrary, Oxford University awarded him an honorary degree in 1907, much to his delight, and some of his staunchest advocates and most sensitive readers both in his time and in ours have been British. One thinks of [British author] Andrew Lang, for example, who in 1887 deemed Twain "one of the greatest living geniuses" and chastised cultured critics in the United States for being "not as proud of Mark Twain" as they ought to be. In the twentieth century, [British author] Tony Tanner's brilliant readings of Twain come to mind, as do fine recent critical studies by Peter Messent and Peter Stoneley, all of whom appreciate Twain's efforts to write a book unlike any that had gone before. This was, of course, precisely what irked the don. His attitude resonates with the irritation Tom Sawyer expressed toward Huck in *Huckleberry Finn:* "You don't ever seem to want to do anything that's regular," Tom complained, "you want to be starting something fresh all the time." An Englishman, Twain once observed, "is a person who does things because they have been done before." An American, he maintained, is "a person who does things because they haven't been done before."

"What is it that confers the noblest delight?," Twain asked in *The Innocents Abroad.*

> What is that which swells a man's breast with pride above that which any other experience can bring to him? . . . To be the *first*—that is the idea. To do something, say something, see something, before *any body* else—these are the things that confer a pleasure compared with which other pleasures are tame and commonplace, other ecstasies cheap and trivial.

Mark Twain was indeed able to "do something, say something, see something before any body else": he saw the imaginative possibilities the United States offered, and his acts and words and visions changed the literary landscape forever. He disrupted familiar paradigms, smashed stale pieties, and blasted any dogma or system he found in his way. The wildness, the anarchic irreverence, the hilarity and the élan were antidotes to the self-satisfied conventionality, ordered seriousness, and grim purposefulness that Twain knew could be fatal to the development of a "sound heart."

Mark Twain helped his readers extricate themselves from the sensibilities of the Victorian era and begin the march toward modernity. He helped writers narrow the gap between the oral and the written and learn to capture vernacular speech on the page with unprecedented spirit and grace. He modeled how a writer could probe the complexities of contemporary challenges without losing the storyteller's sense of narrative or drama. He did all this in language that was clear, sharp, and meticulously crafted—and he demanded from those around him nothing less.

Mark Twain may not have suspected, when he set off on the *Quaker City* voyage in 1867 that would produce *The Innocents Abroad*, that the journey would mark a milestone in American cultural navigation. The great explorers of the past had planted European flags on the soil of the New World. Twain sailed back the other way and figuratively planted an American flag on the European continent, marking as his own an imaginative terrain that the native inhabitants had for centuries assumed was theirs.

Europe was rich with everything America had none of: castles; relics; royalty; history; ancient legends; certifiably "great" painters, sculptors, composers, and writers. For Europeans, indeed, for most Americans who preceded Twain as travelers to Europe, the proper stance for an American in the face of the grandeur that was Europe was awestruck admiration. But time and time again Twain refused to genuflect on command. He tells us, for example, that the guide in Genoa

> had something which he thought would overcome us. He said: "Ah, genteelmen, you come wis me! I show you beautiful, O, magnificent bust Christopher Colombo!—splendid, grand, magnificent!' . . .
>
> The doctor put up his eye-glass—procured for such occasions:
>
> "Ah, what did you say this gentleman's name was?"
>
> "Christopher Colombo!—great Christopher Colombo!"
>
> "Christopher Colombo—the great Christopher Colombo. Well, what did *he* do?"
>
> "Discover America!—discover America, Oh, ze devil!"
>
> "Discover America. No—that statement will hardly wash. We are just from America ourselves. We heard nothing about it. Christopher Colombo—pleasant name—is—is he dead?"

As Twain debunks both an Old World icon and the sanctity of crediting Europe with the "discovery" of America, the famous "is he dead?" line resonates with the larger trope of

European culture as centered on a dead past and American culture as centered on a living present. Twain did not invent the "is he dead?" joke, but he brought it to new heights. "Guides cannot master the subtleties of the American joke," Twain tells us. He celebrated his compatriots' limberness of mind while taking potshots at acolytes of the Old World's ossified artifacts. Like Huck, who "don't take no stock in dead people," Mark Twain and his fellow travelers have limited patience for celebrating dead heroes of European manifest destiny. They are more concerned with capturing new territory across the Atlantic as a province of the American imagination. In *The Innocents Abroad* Mark Twain took on the challenge of making the world safe for an art hewn from the untrammeled, freewheeling vernacular language of his native land.

REJECTING THE VICTORIAN AESTHETIC

To clear the way for the success of his own artistic endeavors, Twain had to train his readers to reject the sentimental claptrap that often figured prominently in their notions of "art." For a young man named Grant Wood, who would become one of the best known realist painters of the twentieth century, this strategy provided an epiphany. Wood vividly recalled from his childhood reading of *Huckleberry Finn*

> the part wherein Huck, staying with the Grangerfords, describes the sentimental pictures a daughter in the family had painted before her premature death. "They was different from any pictures I ever see before—" Huck said, "Blacker, mostly, than is common." And of all the pictures, you will remember the masterpiece was an unfinished study of a grief-stricken young woman ready to leap off a bridge, tears, gown and hair flowing with three pairs of arms—all in different positions. The idea had been to see which pair of arms would look the best and then to scratch out the other two, but the young artist had died before she had made up her mind. "The young woman in the picture," Huck remarked, "had a kind of nice, sweet face but there was so many arms it made her look too spidery, it seemed to me."

> As I look back on it now, I realize that my response to this passage was a revelation. Having been born into a world of Victorian standards, I had accepted and admired the ornate, the lugubrious and the excessively sentimental naturally and without questions. And this was my first intimation that there was something ridiculous about sentimentality.

Wood believes his life was changed by his exposure to "the

brave way in which—in an age of submission" Mark Twain "lashed out against the artificialities and false standards of his time."

In a similar vein, [American author] Bobbie Ann Mason maintains that Twain's "plain style assaulted the wordy romantic rubbish of his day." At a time when "flowery writing"—concentrations of "too many big, unfamiliar and empty words"—had scared many ordinary readers away from "literature," Mason writes, "Twain was one of the first writers in America to deflower literary language." In place of "wordy romantic rubbish" Twain often gives us what Mason calls "rigged-up language," a "language that functions through its potential for inventiveness, just as the necessities of the frontier called for ingenious solutions—making do with what was at hand." Mason, who hails from Kentucky, the state in which Twain's parents were raised, finds this inventiveness deliciously familiar. But precisely what Mason values can strike British purists as beneath respect. As [Canadian author] Mordecai Richler reminds us, in March 1995 Prince Charles, speaking at the British Council's English 2000 project,

> warned against the threat to "proper English" from the spread of the American vernacular, which he pronounced very corrupting. Because of American influence, he said, "People tend to invent all sorts of nouns and verbs, and make words that shouldn't be. I think we have to be a bit careful, otherwise the whole thing can get rather a mess."

"Obviously Prince Charles has never read Mark Twain . . . or Twain's successors," Richler notes, "and is unaware of how they have enriched a living language that is constantly evolving." He recommends that Prince Charles immediately be sent a copy of *The Innocents Abroad.* Despite the desire of an occasional don or prince to wish it away, Mark Twain's influence on the English language is undeniable and vast. Indeed, Twain is cited in the most recent edition of the *Oxford English Dictionary* more than eighteen hundred times.

If Twain helped clear away the floridly ornate Victorian prose style and invigorated the language with new verbal inventions he also, in *Huckleberry Finn* and other works, ushered into the house of letters a new kind of narrator: someone who spoke in dialect but who was nonetheless authorized to be the central consciousness of the story. Twain dissociated the notion of being good from the capacity to use good grammar. Indeed, in *Huckleberry Finn* the morally base king and duke have some of the "best" speech in the book. Critics have suggested that such memorable twentieth-century narrators as J.D. Salinger's Holden Caulfield in *Catcher in the Rye* or Alice Walker's Celie in *The Color Purple* may be distant relatives of Huckleberry Finn—along with the narrators of Sherwood Anderson's "I Want to Know Why" and Albert Murray's *Train Whistle Guitar,* or Lee Smith's multiple first-person narrators in *Oral History.* Twain's most recent literary legacy in the vernacular narrator department is a fourteen-year-old abused child who is the central consciousness of Russell Banks's gripping 1995 novel *Rule of the Bone.* Bone's observant and sharp first-person narration is slangy, immediate, and engaging. In addition, Bone, like Huck, lacks both self-awareness and self-pity and tries to tell the truth. . . .

THE VOICE OF AMERICAN LITERATURE

Twain helped instill in his fellow writers a respect for clarity and precision in language and an appreciation of what that clarity and precision could yield. For a number of major authors in the twentieth century he became the ultimate writing teacher. . . . He understood that the best defense against tyranny was laughter, and that the best vaccine against despair was hope. He insisted on taking America seriously. And he insisted on *not* taking America seriously: "I think that there is but a single specialty with us, only one thing that can be called by the wide name 'American,'" he once wrote. "That is the national devotion to ice-water."

Mark Twain understood the nostalgia for a "simpler" past that increased as that past receded—and he saw through that nostalgia to a past that was just as conflicted and complex as the present. He held out to us an invitation to enter that past and learn from it. Are we strong enough to accept?

Twain threw back at us our dreams and our denial of those dreams, our greed, our goodness, our ambition, and our laziness, all rattling around together in that vast echo chamber of our talk—that sharp, spunky American talk that Mark Twain figured out how to write down without robbing it of its energy and immediacy—talk shaped by voices that the official arbiters of "culture" deemed of no importance: voices of children, voices of slaves, voices of servants, voices of ordinary people. Mark Twain listened. And he made us listen. To the stories he told us and to the truths they conveyed. May he continue to goad us, chasten us, delight us, berate us, and cause us to erupt in unrestrained laughter in unexpected places.

Mark Twain's Satire

Eric Mottram

In the following essay, Eric Mottram notes that Mark Twain's first works were written during the promising post–Civil War era, amid booming industrialization and urban development. With a strong belief in the triumph of his nation's morality, Twain touted the enterprising, unpretentious American identity, and contrasted it humorously with that of stuffy, class-conscious Europeans. However, Mottram suggests, Twain came to believe that the industrial boom in America had led to unchecked material greed and political corruption, and that the American people were in fact morally ambivalent about such matters. His faith shaken, Twain began to suspect that morality was really nothing more than social conditioning, rather than an innate human quality, and that the only constants among humans were tyranny and ignorance. Mottram discusses Twain's disillusionment as it is expressed in the satire of his later works, noting that Twain found it increasingly difficult to write from within the confines of his humorous persona, given the depth of his pessimistic resignation about the fate of America, and indeed, the human race itself. Eric Mottram is Professor of English at King's College in the University of London.

The humorist's character, and his constant exposure to audience response of the most dictating kind, makes him peculiarly sensitive to the complexity of his society. But he has none of the false objectivity of the academic sociologist, and attempts to turn Twain into . . . some mystical priest of the American heartlands—notoriously by such as [T.S.] Eliot and [Lionel] Trilling—have failed. No such simplification is possible. He is self-consciously and violently aware of America in its post-Civil War necessities of recovery, but

Excerpted from "A Raft Against Washington: Mark Twain's Criticism of America," by Eric Mottram, in *Mark Twain: A Sumptuous Variety*, edited by Robert Giddings (Totowa, NJ: Barnes & Noble, 1985). Reprinted with the permission of the Mottram Archives, King's College London. Endnotes in the original have been omitted in this reprint.

distrusts human action in any society. *The Adventures* of *Huckleberry Finn* (1885) can be read as subversion of America in so many ways that it is repeatedly banned from libraries and schools. Senator [Joseph] McCarthy himself joined the parade which, in 1957, included the Board of Education of New York City, and in 1982, the Mark Twain Intermediate School, Fairfax County, Virginia. Twain's analysis of hypocrisy is feared by any authority, and his analysis of behaviour without recourse to religious or philosophic authority. His understanding of repressive law, written and unwritten, is penetrating. In an essay on 'The Jewish question' his bases are sardonically expressed enough to antagonize any limited humanist:

> I am quite sure that (bar one) I have no race prejudices, and I think I have no colour prejudices nor caste prejudices nor creed prejudices, indeed I know it. I can stand any society. All that I care to know is that a man is a human being—that is enough for me. He can't be any worse.

In old age, his satirical pamphlet entitled *King Leopold's Soliloquy* concerns the wholesale massacre and rape of Congo Africans by Belgians under Leopold II, who posed as a colonial philanthropist and a great Christian. Twain points out that between 1897 and 1907 the population was reduced by 3,000,000 people mutilated or killed in one small region in six months. The American satirist attacked where few others were even aware of an intolerable situation—he has Leopold make what was to be the perpetual complaint of the oppressor in the twentieth century:

> (Studies some photographs of mutilated Negroes—throws them down. Sighs.) The kodak has been a sore calamity to us. . . . In the early years we had no trouble in getting the press to 'expose' the tales of the mutilations as slanders, lies, inventions of busybody American missionaries and exasperated foreigners who had found the 'open door' of the Berlin-Congo charter closed against them when they innocently went out there to trade; and by the press's help we got the Christian nations everywhere to turn an irritated and unbelieving ear to those tales and say hard things about the tellers of them. Yes, all things went harmoniously and pleasantly in those good days. . . . Then all of a sudden came the crash! That is to say, the incorruptible *kodak*—and all the harmony went to hell! The only witness I have encountered in my long experience that I couldn't bribe.

At least in his *public* old age, Twain maintained that the human race could still turn away from atrocities, and that

the kodak would be instrumental against the world's
Leopolds and their crusades. Huckleberry Finn had already
encountered Tom Sawyer's definitions of 'crusader' in *Tom
Sawyer Abroad* (1894)—a character already the type of the
American trimmer or liberal who can live with the idea that
it is 'religious to go and take the land from people that owns
it'. 'Bible Teaching and Religious Practice', which only appeared in 1923, exposes the gap between 'human decency'
and religious theory and practice among Christians. The exposure of the ludicrous results of taking the Bible literally,
Letters from the Earth, was written in 1909, the year before
his death, but not published until 1962. Twain realized that
religion was both tyrannical and unnecessary, that human
existence constituted its own hell without inventing another
(Jonson's point in *The Devil Is an Ass*)—but that it could be
dangerous to say so publicly in a society so aggressively,
self-righteously orthodox. Penetrating further, at the end of
his life, the sheer pettiness of local morality faded for him
before the immensity of the godless universe and its facts of
death. His vision concerned the monstrosity of life itself. . . .

Twain once wrote: 'Every man is a moon, and has a dark
side which he never shows to anybody.' In his 1899 sketch
'What Is Man?', his sceptical relativism and sense of the absurd pathos of dogma is clear:

> There are none but temporary Truth-seekers; . . . a perma-
> nent [truth] is a human impossibility; . . . as soon as the
> Seeker finds what he is thoroughly convinced is Truth, he
> seeks no further, but gives up the rest of his days to hunting
> junk to patch it and caulk it and prop it up with, and make it
> weatherproof and keep it from caving in on him.

Scepticism obviates the easy mind both privately and publicly. Doubleness of name is matched by duplicity of creative work. But Twain's is the characteristic unease of the
modern writer whose awareness of hypocrisy and cruelty
does not cause him to retreat entirely into privacy or into
suicide, but rather commits him to a writing of controlled
hysteria. Twain was composing 'Captain Stormfield's Visit
to Heaven' as early as 1868, but his wife forbade publication and it did not appear until after her death in 1907, and
then only in extracts. The story registers a turn-of-the-
century experience of the overwhelming immensity of time
and space under the pressures of nineteenth-century
analysis of the infinities of a universe which had become

what [historian] Henry Adams in 1906 termed a multi-verse. At the end of a century of American developments in science fiction Twain's captain journeys in space-time to a Heaven which proves to be a ghastly conventional replica of Earth societies, confirming, as it were, Huck Finn's worse intuitions of 'civilization'. Heaven is an aristocratic state, the eternal hierarchy that human beings are unable to resist as their ideal—the Washington 'paradise' of *The Gilded Age.* Sandy McWilliams, the captain's guide, points up the eternal aristocratism of Christianity, to which, of course, Americans thoroughly adhered:

> How are you going to have a republic under a king? How are you going to have a republic at all, where the head of government is absolute, holds his place forever, and has no parliament, no counsel to meddle or make in his affairs, nobody voted for, nobody elected, nobody asked to take a hand in its matters, and nobody *allowed* to do it? . . . This is Russia—only more so. There is no shadow of a republic about it anywhere. There are ranks here.

A slight shift and we are in the satirical world of Stanley Elkin's *The Living Earth* in 1980. But *The Gilded Age* already indicated Twain's scepticism about the voting and jury systems, and he is by no means consistently against Hank Morgan's industrial labour state imposed on King Arthur's Christian monarchy.

In 'To a Person Sitting in Darkness', which he managed to publish in the liberal and respected *North American Review* in 1901, Twain, like [Herman] Melville before him, exposed the hypocrisy of Christian colonial aggression, turning from the rottenness of American cities to the international example of cruel exploitation, the greed of missionary organization in China, England's Boer War, the Germans in Africa, and American policy in Cuba. His bitter irony moves into the style of a man under moral pressure, whose sense of outrage is anarchic rather than ideological—the contained anger of a man without 'a permanent truth'. On 30 December 1900, Twain, the celebrated public figure largely assumed to be a humorist and therefore relatively harmless, contributed a New Year greeting, to readers of the New York *Herald*, as from the nineteenth to the twentieth century:

> I bring you the stately matron named Christendom, returning bedraggled, besmirched and dishonoured from pirate raids on Kiaou-Chou, Manchuria, South Africa, and the Philippines, with her soul full of meanness, her pocket full of boodle and

her mouth full of pious hypocrisies. Give her soap and a towel, but hide the looking-glass.

"WHAT IS MAN?"

But why should she not be confronted with her own savage image? Apparently because Twain withdraws from the entropic chaos of the possible results. A year earlier, in 'What Is Man?', Twain proposed—and it is part of that behaviourist materialism which dominates [the fiction of] both Theodore Dreiser and B.F. Skinner later in the century—man as a chemical machine, helpless within its determinations. This side of the sketch's polemic is provided by the Old Man, who is opposed by a Young Man with untried optimistic moral assumptions of a vaguely Christian humanist sentimentality. The dialogue is completely biased. The Old Man crushes the Young Man with a model of human existence determined by forces which reduce original ideas and freedom of will in the historically persisted manner of Jonathan Edwards in the eighteenth century and Hemingway, with his 'biological trap', in the twentieth:

> A man's brain is so constructed that it can originate nothing whatever. . . . It has no command over itself, its owner has no command over it. . . . Inestimably valuable is training, influence, education, in right directions—training one's self-approbation to elevate its ideals.

The Young Man protests: What about self-sacrifice?— but when he is challenged can find no instances. A man's impulse is solely to 'content his own spirit . . . and winning its approval'; he loves 'the approval of his neighbours and the public' more than peace. War occurs because 'public opinion could force some men to do anything.' Twain attacks, therefore, the bases of consensus opinion in the controls of democracy in America—and goes further. [Ralph Waldo] Emerson's doctrine of self-reliance in America, supported by an overweening transcendentalist optimism, becomes an automatism; men do not create or think, they imitate—'wit-mechanism . . . is automatic in its action', and cannot be manufactured—'men observe and combine, that is all. So does a rat.' Instinct is simply 'petrified thought' and 'fleas can be taught nearly anything that a Congressman can.' The impulse instigating these opinions lies within a statement whose variations may be found throughout Twain's work:

The fact that man knows right from wrong proves his *intellectual* superiority to the other creatures; but the fact that he can *do* wrong proves his *moral* inferiority to any creature that cannot.

But, says the Old Man, one does not publish such opinions because

it is a desolating doctrine; it is not inspiring, enthusing, uplifting. It takes the glory out of man, it takes the pride out of him, it takes the heroism out of him, it denies him all personal credit, all applause.

As for nations, they feel rather than think:

They get their feelings at second-hand through their temperaments, not their brains. A nation can be brought—by force of circumstances, not argument—to reconcile itself to any kind of government or religion that can be devised; in time it wills itself to the required conditions; later, it will prefer them and will fiercely fight for them.

To the Young Man's dismay and alarm, he offers finally: 'Everything has been tried. Without success. I beg you not to be troubled.' It could easily be argued that such a dogmatic enclosure, with its grid fitted tightly over any future, is a spiteful recommendation to endless obedience to Control in all its manifestations against imaginative invention. But within all Twain's work, whatever the strategies of humour, lies this stoic resignation, the melancholy of a non-revolutionary writing after his country's Civil War disaster, and as part of a determinist rejection of the genteel belief in America's self-confidence. 'The Facts Concerning the Recent Carnival of Crime in Connecticut' (1875) probe deeply into the capitalist ethic itself as it seethes in ambivalence at the basis of the American way of life. . . .

"THE MAN THAT CORRUPTED HADLEYBURG"

Just over twenty years later, between 1898 and 1900, Twain wrote one of his most accomplished short fictions on the nature of honesty as an assumed value. 'The Man That Corrupted Hadleyburg' essentially dramatizes what [John] Milton called 'a blank virtue'. The town has a reputation for honesty—a social fact of relationship which has to be kept up. Vanity, in characteristic puritan fashion, is disguised as uprightness never put to the extreme test. Practical morality or ethical behaviour appears to cover both selfishness and self-approval. A destitute man was once helped by a Hadleyburg citizen and given twenty dollars—with which he gambles and makes a fortune. Now he wishes to repay the help anonymously, and the citizen can do what he likes with the huge sum of money accumulated from speculation. To the Hadleyburg people it is 'the wages of sin'. Edward Richards turns out to be a man living in the glamour of false reputation for goodness, concealing meanness and profound dishonesty as expediency. Mary Richards prays 'Lead us not into temptation' but only as a superstitious ritual before being tempted. When gold offers itself, Edward says it is the act of Providence whose designs must not be challenged—that would be 'blasphemous presumption'. Where, in 'What Is Man?', the Old Man claimed behaviour is training, and, in *A Connecticut Yankee*, Twain asserted 'Training is everything; training is all there is *to* a person. . . . We have no thoughts of our own, no opinions of our own; they are transmitted to us, trained into us', here Mary Richards rebels against the training with which the town maintains its reputation:

> It's been one everlasting training and training and training in honesty—honesty shielded, from the cradle, against every possible temptation, and so it's artificial honesty, as weak as water when temptation comes, as we have seen this night. . . . Let no man call me honest again—I will not have it.

So the people refuse to be honest in order to save their souls: 'the weakest of all weak things is a virtue which has not been tested in the fire.' Twain reserves his sharpest attack for the man who is not worried by sin unless other people discover his condition and destroy his reputation. His main figure is so corrupted by concealed sin that he becomes half-crazed with its intensity. But the text contains no compassion for human moral dilemma. Twain leaves the town praying 'Lead us into temptation' and thereby, of course, challenging the Lord's Prayer, whose very title is authoritarian and aristocratic and therefore reflected back into Captain Stormfield's Heaven. Twain once remarked that the symbol of man ought to be an axe, 'for every human being has one concealed about him somewhere, and is always seeking the opportunity to grind it.'

In *Innocents Abroad*, the work through which he first received popular approval in 1869, Twain proposes American values of comfort, utility, and progress itself with a dashing confidence, exposing culture-snobs and culture-seekers in Europe and boosting American morale as a post–Civil War journalist. He began, that is, in a period of heavy city development and industrialization, the hypocrisies of Social Darwinism condoning poverty and wealth by natural selection, the domination of high-finance capitalism and those forms of determinism and stoicism which contributed to the naturalist novel in [Stephen] Crane and [Theodore] Dreiser. By 1873 and *The Gilded Age*, Twain—only four years later—is drawn to the Jonsonian exposure of national political and social corruption, the absurdly dangerous visions of horizonless material progress and the urge to irresistible power—the subject of Edmund Wilson's *Patriotic Gore*. . . .

A CONNECTICUT YANKEE IN KING ARTHUR'S COURT

For *A Connecticut Yankee in King Arthur's Court*, sixteen years later, Twain reworks those materials of Arthurian chivalry and medieval church authority—used by writers as diverse as [Lord] Tennyson, T.S. Eliot and Jean Cocteau—to analyse the technological environment of late nineteenth-century America, accepted uncritically by the mass of Americans. He had already mocked the chivalric pretensions of the Southern ruling classes in *Life on the Mississippi* (1883), a work which also presents the dandy paragon of training, the riverboat pilot Horace Bixby. Now he transfers Hank Morgan, mechanic at the Colt factory in Hartford, Connecticut—a major and highly imitated centre of the American method of manufacture (especially the semi-mechanical assembly of duplicated and replaceable parts)—to feudal Britain. He trains the backward British into a paternalistic technological utopia of Americanism, complete with advertising and advanced weaponry.

Once again, Twain's humour only just controls his exacerbated nerves, his outrage with tyranny and his disgust with human stupidity. Hank is to be the American Franklinite pragmatist of materialism, the kind-hearted Boss. Merlin is cast as magic power over the people by ritual and muddled beliefs. Slaves are those workers and poor stupid enough not to rebel. Hank brings industrialism, the new Grail, wage-labour colonization. Twain's ambivalence is not at all concealed. Hank tells the people: 'I'm going to turn groping and grumbling automata into *men*.' Self-reliance geared into the factory system is intended to create a limited peaceful revolution. Aristocratism is exemplified by the absurd discomforts and impracticability of grotesque suits of armour—a scene both hilarious and painful in Twain's most characteristic manner. But Hank's reformed knights become salesmen advertising soap and toothbrushes, agents of the system Twain elsewhere excoriates.

This novel, like *Huckleberry Finn* and *Pudd'nhead Wilson,* is structured as a dialectic between the cruel and the ridiculous, between degradation and dignity, the pathetic and the stupid, illusion and reality. But Twain transfers the earlier American beliefs in anarchic self-reliance and pragmatic inventiveness at the service of society to an industrial context which drains them of vitality. Hank's factories are 'iron and steel missionaries of future civilization'. He believes revolutions begin in a bloody 'Reign of Terror' and end in technological beneficence. Scepticism directs the plot; Hank may be 'the champion of hard, unsentimental common sense' but he is outwitted by Merlin magic plus the Church. He blows up his technocracy, dynamites and electrocutes 25,000 knights, and kills off his own retinue with the resultant polluted air. Then he leaves these members of 'the damned human race' to fry, as Twain uses his own fictioneer's magic to waft him back to isolationist Hartford.

Hysterical and accurate cynicism also motivates *Pudd'n-head Wilson* (1894), a thorough damnation of social hierarchy and its peculiarly American yearning to imitate European class society, and of the cruel absurdities of racism and slavery. Dawson's Landing is the provincial core of the damned in the heart of America's Mississippi artery lands. The plot articulates ironic despair with the centre of the would-be democratic—Hadleyburg, Eseldorf in *The Mysterious Stranger,* and here a Mississippi small town, a place of overlapping farce and tragedy. The plot's complexities of duplicity constitute the form of the entangled superstition and violence within American small-town hypocrisy and hierarchy, where law is for ever a frontier instability—as it is in the Arkansas town in *Huckleberry Finn* where Colonel Sherburn and Bloggs try to fight it out. The novel is a post–Civil War text on slavery, aristocratism and democratic idiocy. The bloody war had been no lesson, is part of the message. . . .

THE MYSTERIOUS STRANGER

In 1898 Twain produced *The Mysterious Stranger* and hid it. Four years after *Pudd'nhead Wilson* he had reached a chronic division between private writing and public distribution, a schizophrenic separation of private pessimism and public image as comedian. The angel Satan's final words to

Theodore Fischer, the narrator, extend 'What Is Man?' into the blackness of *The Great Dark:*

> It is true that which I have revealed to you; there is no God, no universe, no human race, no earthly life, no heaven, no hell. It is all a dream—a grotesque and foolish dream. Nothing exists but you. And you are but a thought, a homeless thought, wandering forlorn among the empty eternities!

Fischer knows he is right, and no Young Man's protest is available. The 1590 Austrian scene is a private and determined hell of Twain's invention, and the plot demonstrates the meaninglessness of moral sense, choice and human dignity. Freedom is to be 'alone in shoreless space, to wander in its limitless solitudes without friend or comrade for ever', and to realize that this *is* the human condition. The angel shows Theodore all history as a brutal competitiveness, a gilded age stretching back into time, in which man's moral sense enables him to choose murder, war and mutual exploitation.

Twain's turn-of-the-century wounded optimism has become a grid of gloom. He is concerned with no systematic philosophic or historical analysis. Once again men are imaged as ants in the control of a superior force—a long American line from Jonathan Edwards to *A Farewell to Arms* and 'Big Two-Hearted River'—and their environment is proposed as a fixture. Community and mutual aid are impossible. Psychology is a pleasure-pain structure of tension and release. In Chapter 7, Twain writes 'God has forsaken us.' But where for Nietzsche contemporaneously, and Camus later, this is a signal to move forwards into a consideration of the existential situation, for Twain it is a signal for despair. His prose begins to lack the energy of his finest fictions and essays, and explicitly, in Chapter 10, man's sense of humour, once a powerful weapon, is now 'lying rusting' because he lacks 'sense and courage':

> Power, money, persuasion, supplication, persecution—these can lift a colossal humbug—push it a little—weaken it a little, century after century, but only laughter can blow it to rags and atoms at a blast. Against the assault of laughter nothing can stand.

That strength has become virtually impossible for Twain; in Chapter 10 he writes:

> No sane man can be happy, for to him life is real and he sees what a fearful thing it is. Only the mad can be happy, and not many of those. . . . Of course, no man is entirely in his own right mind at any time, but I have been referring to the extreme cases.

After Twain, such a delineation became nearly a common-place—summarized by the great humorist James Thurber in two aphorisms: 'There is no safety in numbers, or in anything else' and 'Run, don't walk, to the nearest exit.' The limits of humour in America were still being pressed hard by the 'black humorists' during the Civil Rights conflict and the imperialism of the 1960s and 1970s, and by the farce and tragedy which destabilize the masterly plot of William Eastlake's *Dancers in the Scalp House.* The beautiful affirmations of *The Adventures of Huckleberry Finn* in 1885 were unique in Twain's career—a 12-year-old uneducated boy's self-reliance and self-release from the society he is trained to inherit and believe: family, religion, law, racism, the system of that civilizated duplicity and its disasters.

CHAPTER 4

Mark Twain's Legacy

PEOPLE
WHO MADE
HISTORY

MARK TWAIN

The Mark Twain Phenomenon

Glenn Collins

Glenn Collins considers the enduring popularity of Mark Twain in American society nearly a century after his death, citing such recent evidence as the release of a $6 million, three-dimensional IMAX film about his life, two documentaries about his work by the Public Broadcasting Service, and the appearance of dozens of websites run by dedicated Mark Twain buffs. Mark Twain is frequently featured as a character on television shows and in fiction, and even has monuments and amusement parks named after him outside the U.S. Collins notes that scholars attribute the Mark Twain phenomenon to, among other things, his wicked wit and subversiveness, and to the fact that he grappled with issues that are still very much a concern in society, including race relations, animal rights, and the implications of technological progress. Glenn Collins is a reporter for *The New York Times.*

Here now in the high noon of fence-whitewashing season, when civilized people like Becky Thatcher and Aunt Polly might seek refuge in the shade of a porch, comes the latest Imax adventure. It's colorful, noisy, globe-trotting three-dimensional celebration of—Mark Twain?

Yes, Samuel Langhorne Clemens, who adopted the pen name Mark Twain, will take his place on the eight story-tall screen, superseding the flicker of previous Imax extravaganzas that have portrayed the quest for the summit of Everest, the hunt for the Titanic and the pedal-stomping proclivities of professional race car drivers.

Indeed, the premiere of the film, "Mark Twain's America in 3-D," in Manhattan is a testament to the continuing mass ap-

Reprinted, with permission, from "Twain Rolls On to New Heights," by Glenn Collins, *The New York Times,* July 15, 1998, pp. E1, E3. Copyright © 1998 by The New York Times Co.

peal of the cynosure of [Twain's hometown of] Hannibal, Missouri. Improbably, 88 years after his death and 122 years after the publication of "The Adventures of Tom Sawyer," America is sustaining a Twain boom that betrays no sign of abating.

"His popularity is growing," said Shelley Fisher Fishkin, professor of American studies and English at the University of Texas at Austin, the editor of the 29-volume "The Oxford Mark Twain" (1996). "Twain scholarship is increasing, articles are coming out by the dozens, there are new films in the works, and Twain is the subject of exchanges on the Internet."

Researchers say the Twain phenomenon—fueled by the author's wicked wit, enduring seductiveness and flat-out subversiveness—keeps captivating audiences in each new generation. Twain himself put it this way: "My books are water; those of the great geniuses are wine. Everybody drinks water."

Nonetheless, said Justin Kaplan, a Twain biographer: "It is too easy to sentimentalize him as the foxy grandpa of American letters, the author of wholesome books for the young. Twain was a man with an extremely dark imagination and a low threshold of annoyance." Mr. Kaplan won the Pulitzer Prize and the National Book Award for his study, "Mr. Clemens and Mark Twain."

To some scholars, the 20th century bears the mark of Twain. They see the current nostalgic hoopla over this Victorian as an emblem of the intense millennial preoccupation with the 19th century.

But though that era has been idealized as the golden age of invention, exploration, colonization and the mass industry that fueled a pivotally unifying civil war, Twain grappled with many of the messy issues that still torment the fin-de-siècle American psyche.

"As the millennium approaches," Dr. Fishkin said, "scholars are looking back a century ago and seeing Twain as a truth-teller. There is virtually no issue on the horizon right now that Twain didn't deal with then, in his work." The roster includes animal rights, the impact of technology, the tension between heredity and environment, the boundaries of gender and the interracial debate.

A century and a half after the famously riverine Twain worked as a printer's apprentice in Hannibal, he has Java-star status on the Internet. For example, the Mark Twain Forum (reachable through many search engines) provides information of interest to Twainians, as Clemens buffs call themselves.

It offers links to dozens of Twain sites including the Mining Company Guide (http://marktwain.miningco.com/), which posts the latest Twain flashes, like the movement in Manila to celebrate Philippine-American Friendship Day by building a Mark Twain monument, or the popularity of juvenile horse-riding in a Japanese amusement park called the Tom Sawyer Bokuju.

There are also Internet bulletins about the latest attempts to banish "Huckleberry Finn" from bookstores and library shelves, including the recent move by the Pennsylvania State Conference of the National Association for the Advancement of Colored People to remove the novel from required-reading lists in the state's schools.

OFTEN SHOWING UP AS HIMSELF IN FICTION

The public television station WGBH in Boston is preparing a documentary on "Huckleberry Finn," and Ken Burns—of baseball, Lewis and Clark and Civil War fame—is working on a two-part Twain documentary to appear on PBS in 2001; even a Hollywood producer is approaching Twain scholars for advice on an animated Twain movie.

So powerful is the Twain presence that contemporary writers have made him a character in their fiction. They include Gore Vidal, in his novel "1876"; Joyce Carol Oates in her novel "A Bloodsmoor Romance"; the "Riverworld" series by the science fiction author Philip Jose Farmer, and the Mark Twain mysteries of Peter J. Heck, author of "Death on the Mississippi."

And not only was Twain a character in "Bonanza" and "Cheers," but also a time-travel episode was built about Twain on "Star Trek: The Next Generation."

"Twain has more marquee value than ever," said Mark Katz, a vice president of Sony Pictures Classics, which is distributing the Imax film and is a co-producer.

OLD PHOTOGRAPHS, NEW TECHNIQUES

The Imax documentary—which is told in Twain's words and reaches across two centuries, as did Twain's life—will make its debut on Friday at Sony Theaters Lincoln Square; it will be playing on 10 large-format screens, across the country by the end of the year. The film interweaves the life and times of Twain, as depicted in black-and-white archival photographs, with full-color portrayals of the lives of current-day enthusiasts who revel in the 19th-century Zeitgeist and seek to recreate it.

Its producers see the $6 million Twain film, the first Imax biography, as something of a breakthrough in the evolution of a new entertainment medium. Imax—which, like its predecessor Cinerama, never saw a roller coaster it didn't want

---

 MARK TWAIN TONIGHT!

Hal Holbrook [is] known throughout the world for his one-man show *Mark Twain Tonight!* . . .

The derivation for the show started back in New York City in 1953 when Holbrook was a struggling actor unable to land many roles. Rather than wait on tables, Holbrook decided to create a one-man show about Mark Twain and try to earn money from it. . . .

In 1959 he performed *Mark Twain Tonight!* off-Broadway, and in 1977 brought the show to Broadway, which led to a ninety-minute television special. Twain and Holbrook had become synonymous.

For his efforts as Mark Twain, Holbrook earned a Tony, a Drama Critics' Circle Award, an Obie, and an Emmy, but he is constantly changing, fine-tuning *Mark Twain Tonight!*, adapting it to the times. During the sixties, he used sections from Twain that stressed civil rights; during the seventies, he emphasized Twain's antiwar writings.

Holbrook interprets Twain as "a very sensitive man. He had a keen sense of justice, a strong dislike for lying and for hypocrisy. His values were frontier values—independence, both in thought and action, standing behind your words, dealing with a lot of serious situations by the use of humor."

Having performed his Twain show for over thirty years, Holbrook has come to realize that much of Twain's writing is about one subject—the morality or immorality of man and his actions. "That's at the heart of everything," says the actor. Twain's writing focuses on man's honesty. "Everything relates back to: Do you mean it, or do you don't?" says Holbrook about Twain's sentiments. . . .

Holbrook sees many reasons for the Twain resurgence. After a period of internal unrest based on the Vietnam War and Watergate, Twain represents a return to patriotism. Twain, Holbrook says, as much as any native writer, evokes the independence of the American spirit.

Gary Stern, "Twain Today," *Horizon*, November 1985.

to film—is still dismissed by some as a novelty medium. "But we think of the format as an alternative cinematic art form that is undergoing a maturation process," Mr. Katz said.

Stephen Low, the 3-D film's 47-year-old director, says the documentary allows theatergoers "to look into the eyes of their ancestors and wonder what they were like; these are not actors, and this is not fiction."

Indeed, the 1998 film is based on an extraordinary 19th-century trove of three-dimensional stereopticon negatives from the collection at the University of California-Riverside, California Museum of Photography, many of which present Twain himself, in all his fierce attention, as if he were poised to speak.

The film has been enhanced with archival two-dimensional photographs of the era that have been digitally converted into three-dimensional images. This is believed to be the first time such images have been used on the big screen.

The film appears even as Twain buffs are girding for a summerlong binge of Clemensiana. For example, this weekend the city of Hartford will hold its annual Mark Twain Days festival, with, naturally, cane-pole fishing events, and frog-jumping and fence-painting contests sponsored by the Mark Twain House there.

Thus far the most high-profile Twain bash of the season was mounted on Monday night at the Players, the New York City club that Twain helped found in 1888 and where he lived in 1904. (His pool cue is enshrined in the billiard room.) At a Victorian fund-raiser, 200 guests saw the Imax film, then consumed 19th-century food and were serenaded by banjo, tuba and trombone.

"I never pass up an opportunity to attend an event in my honor," said Mr. Twain himself, greeting the guests in a splendid white suit. When pressed, he allowed that he might be masquerading as an actor by the name Munro Bonnell.

The real Twain "would unleash his barbs at the slightest provocation" at considerable risk to his reputation, said Mr. Kaplan, the biographer. Twain had reason to be provoked, having lost much of his money to unprescient investments, and most of his family to illness. That included his daughter Jean, who died at 29, during an epileptic fit on Christmas Eve. Twain died three months later, in the year of the return of Halley's Comet, 1910: he had been born 75 years before, in 1835, during the year of the comet's previous appearance.

FROM THE RIVERBOAT TO THE AUTOMOBILE

The new documentary portrays Twain as a quintessentially American presence whose life marked the milestones of the 19th century. Twain's arc spanned the era of the riverboat on the Mississippi to that of the motorcar on Fifth Avenue. He fought in the Civil War (briefly, for the South), became wealthy and famous, lost most of his fortune and lived until the era of powered flight.

To be sure, Twain is still a world-class controversy-magnet, not only for the way he refers to blacks in "Huckleberry Finn," but also for his portrayal of female characters.

Some black academics, including Julius Lester, a professor at the University of Massachusetts at Amherst, have adamantly proclaimed Twain's racism, and feminists have charged that his sexism was epitomized by shallow portrayals of women. The novelist Jane Smiley has attributed Twain's grand reputation to the hype generated by a small group of literary critics who canonized "white, Protestant, middle-class male authors."

Other black scholars, like David L. Smith, a professor of English at Williams College, have pointed out that Twain portrayed the interracial friendship of Huck and Jim positively and indicted the ethical myopia of white characters who claimed to be moral while condoning a racist system of law and custom.

"His greatest works have relatively limited roles for female characters, but some of Twain's lesser-known works show a greater range," contended Dr. Fishkin, whose most recent book, "Lighting Out for the Territory" (1997), explores these controversies. "Calling him a sexist or a racist is selling him very short. He was neither."

VIEWS OF PROGRESS AND ITS DARK SIDE

Though Twain once said that "the 20th century is a stranger to me," some see the author's sensibility as especially modern because "he was conflicted, divided, ironic and not at peace with himself," Mr. Kaplan said.

A century before cyberphiles rushed to buy Windows 98, Twain was clearly an early adopter, intrigued by the cutting-edge technologies that produced cash registers, typewriters and photography. He claimed to be the first author in the world to apply a typing machine to literature and proclaimed himself the first book author to use phonographic dictation (for "The American Claimant").

In that 1892 book, he posited a wild-eyed inventor who dreamed up ideas that prefigured the fax machine, the photocopier and DNA cloning. But Twain also wrote about the dark side of progress, envisioning, for example, a technological dystopia in "A Connecticut Yankee in King Arthur's Court."

Not the least of Twain's accomplishments was that he was "wildly funny," Mr. Kaplan said. "This was a man who worshiped laughter as a weapon. Twain was not afraid of *hurting*."

Indeed, "we need Twain now," Mr. Kaplan added with a laugh. "Imagine the kind of satiric and logical intelligence he would apply to the whole Kenneth Starr–Monica Lewinsky business. Twain would be having a ball."

The Enduring Controversy of *Huckleberry Finn*

Kenny J. Williams

Kenny J. Williams evaluates whether *The Adventures of Huckleberry Finn* should be banned from public schools and libraries as some have suggested. At issue is the novel's racial implications, including its use of the pejorative term "nigger" well over a hundred times, as well as what many consider to be a stereotypical rendering of the slave character Jim. Williams acknowledges the offensiveness of the racial epithets, but suggests that the novel cannot be accurately reduced to a simple exercise in name calling. Williams likewise acknowledges Jim's demeaning stereotypical aspects, but argues that he also possesses qualities that elevate him above the level of burlesque, and further, that many of the novel's white characters are imbued with such unflattering traits as ignorance, hypocrisy, and moral ambivalence. Though the novel's inherent contradictions may well be the result of Twain's own moral ambiguity concerning the matter of race, far more important is the fact that they still speak eloquently to the contradictions inherent in America's professed belief in racial equality. To ban the novel, Williams concludes, is to condemn the messenger for the message. Kenny J. Williams is a professor of American literature at Duke University.

No matter what we may wish to tell other nations about ourselves and our American Dream, the ambivalence of many Americans toward matters of race relations remains a factor that is often used to illustrate the hypocrisy of the professed creeds of the United States. If a literary classic is that which

Reprinted, by permission of the author, from *"Adventures of Huckleberry Finn;* or, Mark Twain's Racial Ambiguity," by Kenny J. Williams, *Mark Twain Journal*, vol. 22, no. 2 (Fall 1984), pp. 38–42.

transcends its time and is relevant for the present, the racial implications of *Adventures of Huckleberry Finn*—negative though they are in some respects—may be of value in understanding American civilization. Not only did Mark Twain include overt and subliminal commentary on his own day but he also displayed the uncertainities that have marked the so-called "American dilemma." As we continue to extol the virtue of our democratic experiment to others, the world may well point to our "classic" as evidence of our inherent hypocrisy.

The greatness of *Adventures of Huckleberry Finn* has been accepted without much question. To identify its apparent weaknesses subjects the critic to charges of undue sensitivity or literary naivete. But one does not have to be particularly knowledgeable, for example, to realize that a slave seeking freedom would hardly travel southward on the Mississippi River. Yet, Twain apologists claim that such a concern for historic validity denies the power and license of literary imagination. That other aspects of this realistic novel tax a reader's credulity can be dismissed by those who remind others of Twain's early notice: "Persons attempting to find a motive in this narrative will be prosecuted; persons attempting to find a moral in it will be banished; persons attempting to find a plot in it will be shot." In the end, many considerations of the novel's shortcomings fade before the discussions of its "greatness."

From Ernest Hemingway's declaration ("all modern American literature comes from [it . . . and] it's the best book we've had") to the numerous studies of the novel, *Adventures of Huckleberry Finn* has indeed become part of the folklore of American culture. Throughout the years, critics have cited such elements as Twain's deviation from a genteel tradition that had become artistically stifling in the latter part of the nineteenth century and his picaresque use of the Mississippi River that stresses the symbolic role of that river in American life. Others have pointed to the novel's exploration into such abstract principles as loyalty, morality, freedom, alienation, conscience, and non-compliance to unjust laws to prove merit. Furthermore, in its use of the vernacular, the work unwittingly fulfills Noah Webster's eighteenth-century observation that a national literature would not be created until there was an acceptance of American English as an artistic medium. All of these characteristics suggest that the novel is an outstanding one.

EARLY OBJECTIONS TO THE NOVEL

Twain's chronicle of the adolescent Huck Finn, however, was not without its detractors and doubters even from the beginning. Perhaps no work in American literature has been banned as consistently nor as frequently. Initially, its very points of greatness bothered many. Early arbiters of taste thought stories should be didactic and uplifting. They insisted that tales display a respect for or a commitment to the genteel tradition. Huck was viewed as an inappropriate hero. His language, filled with slang and irreverent allusions with no regard for the rules of grammar, left much to be desired. He was disrespectful of adults and seemed to have little interest in telling the truth. No wonder the prim Louisa May Alcott complained: "If Mr. Clemens cannot think of something better to tell our pure-minded lads and lasses he had better stop writing for them."

Interestingly, but not unexpectedly, Twain's early critics and readers were not exercised about the racial implications of the novel. The Philadelphia Centennial of 1876 had ushered in a new spirit among American painters who recognized not only a need for a continued representation of American subjects but also an obligation, despite the immediate social and political problems, to present in a visual manner the possibilities of American democracy. For many of them, this meant delineations of the newly-freed slaves; nevertheless, even the most tolerant American artists and audiences have had difficulty in dealing with certain phases of our national life despite ardent attempts. In the nineteenth century, most Americans were more comfortable with the portraits drawn by the popular writers and practitioners of the plantation tradition. Although Twain chose to resurrect the antebellum period, the picture of the imagined happy and contented slaves is augmented by Jim who seeks freedom. The other slave characters who appear infrequently seem shadowy reminders of an unaltered plantation tradition.

That there is still some discomfort with Twain's novel is evident from the nature of its defenders and assailants. The focus has shifted. It is Jim, rather than Huck, who presents the problem for some readers. Questions naturally arise. Did Twain use the slave figure in a pejorative way that would have satisfied his audience? Is Jim simply an embodiment of the popular minstrel tradition, or is he in reality an example of "the noble savage"? While apologists for the novel insist upon the "nobility" of Jim, the fact remains that there were (and still are) acceptable stereotypes that appealed (as they do today) to the American public.

Given the racial climate of the late 1870s and the 1880s with its uncontrolled animus, one might wonder what Twain hoped to accomplish. Second-guessing authors has become big business in academe. In fact, there are those who have made entire careers out of merely speculating on the various meanings of a text without necessarily reading it. Indeed, literary reputations have been made and broken on the basis of how well others accept the serious accounts of what so-and-so meant when such-and-such was written. Finding evidence to support various theories is never difficult; hence, these hypotheses and defenses enter into literary criticism. Academicians are not alone in these exercises. The history of book promotion and banning demonstrates that there are those who—like literary critics—select certain aspects of a work to condemn or praise the entire production. Through the years one can find works and/or authors who have especially lent themselves to mis-readings, re-interpretations, and thinly-veiled inquiries. This has often led to overt and covert censorship. And so it has been with Twain's *Adventures of Huckleberry Finn.*

DEFINING THE CENTRAL ISSUES

The earliest censors who believed the novel would corrupt the young have been replaced by later ones who claim the book is racist and degrading. Needless to say, dealing with *Adventures of Huckleberry Finn* on racial grounds creates it own dilemma. To suggest anything on the subject is to run the risk of treading on sensitive ground. One can be accused of narrowness, meanness of spirit, and being amenable to censorship. But to attempt to use the novel as a lesson in tolerance also seems to avoid the central issue in view of the excessive use of the word "nigger" by all of the characters including Jim. (Those who have counted the word's appearance maintain it occurs between 160 and 200 times.) The fact that current editors often explain at length that the term was not as pejorative as modern readers imagine because it was a commonly-used designation for slaves in the 1830s and 1840s does little to lessen its impact. Nor does it give comfort to those students, parents, school boards, and other organizations who question the use of the book in public schools. Clearly, the novel presents a problem for those youngsters who have not had a chance to think through the subtleties of racial epithets. Thus, for many readers there is an implied racism in the novel that does not disappear even when Twain advocates insist the work is a "classic" which should be read.

Some parents and school boards have assumed the deletion of the novel from required reading lists is one viable option. As late as 1984, efforts were made in Springfield, Illinois, to ban the book from the high school curriculum. By im-

This illustration depicts the infamous Huck Finn.

plication there seems to be an acceptance of the notion that to require students to read the novel is to perpetuate its presumed derogatory point of view. Those who would ban it have accepted the argument that students will be embarrassed, hurt, or otherwise damaged. Those who oppose such action assume that blacks can and ought to "understand" the use of a term that is categorized as vulgar and offensive when applied to a Negro.

Implicit in many of the discussions of the novel are some unasked questions about the author. Whether or not Twain was a racist [is] a moot point that does not need to be addressed, although it is amazing to note the number of times readers find it necessary to assert with conviction: "Twain was not a racist." (Some critics apparently believe the statement is sufficiently powerful to dispel any such notion.) I still remember one of my teachers who discussed Jim by explaining in an uncomfortable way that Twain paid the tuitions of some Negro students who attended Yale University. I could never understand the relationship between Jim and those unnamed students, but I suppose it must have had something to do with what Huck might have called "conscience"—Twain's and my teacher's.

I suspected even then that—given the time, the conditions, and his background—Twain's racial attitudes probably did not vary appreciably, at least publicly, from the dominant ones of his day. That he may have become a concerned paternalistic figure like his friend William Dean Howells or that he was to examine slavery sharply and critically in *The Tragedy of Pudd'nhead Wilson* (1894) does not alter the fact that the young Mark Twain served as a Confederate irregular. No matter what he used as a later explanation, his separation from that service had more to do with his desire to go westward than with any strong commitment or switch of loyalties. His knowledge of race, furthermore, was probably limited to a particular group. There is no reason to suppose he would have known much about such [abolitionists] as Maria Stewart, William Hamilton, Joseph Coors, or James Forten. The Missouri of Mark Twain was a cultural world apart from that of John Jones, the [black] multi-millionaire of Chicago, who was making his mark in the financial empires of the Midwest. But in the final analysis, it is the novel—not Twain—that must be reviewed.

If one assumes that the literary classics of a nation represent the ideals, unspoken values, and psychology of a people, *Adventures of Huckleberry Finn* presents some fascinating ambiguities. On one level, there is the possibility of viewing the novel in terms of the [Ralph Waldo Emerson's] doctrine of self-reliance, the freedom of the spirit, the dignity of humanity that cannot be enslaved, and the ultimate note of optimism that emphasizes the ability "to light out for [new] Territory ahead of the rest." Yet, the novel gives mixed signals on matters of race. The slave characters are, for the most part, undeveloped stereotypes who perform within the mandates of the plantation tradition. Mention of a free black appears in the context of Pap's diatribe against the "govment." While sophisticated readers may dismiss Pap as part of the "ornery" ones, the fact remains that he repeats a widely-held denigration of blacks believed by those who object to a Negro's dress, education, right to vote, and claims to freedom. The history of American race relations reveals that Pap was not alone in such complaints. Furthermore, the people of the novel are essentially the poor whites and rogues of the Mississippi Valley. Colonel Sherburn clearly is of a better class, but readers meet him during an act of violence. The Grangerfords and Shepherdsons are presented through their mindless feud; but they are also in a state of decline as is the Wilks family. With the exception of Jim, it is a fairly sorry lot of people.

Assessing Jim

And what of Jim? Much can be made of reducing the adult black male to a figure whose fate rests with an unlettered white teenager. Others might argue that Jim's status is a condescending reminder of that "peculiar institution," forgetting in the process that tales of slavery represent historic fact as well as form a popular literary tradition among those readers who find the work of such writers as Joel Chandler Harris to be a valid portrait of the ante-bellum period. (In the twentieth century, the popularity of slave romances and Margaret Mitchell's *Gone With The Wind*, 1936, suggests that the image of the mythical Old South still lives.) Some readers may decry Jim's superstitious nature and take his reliance upon "signs" as an indication of his backwardness. Forgetting that these folkways—like all such customs—explain the inexplicable to primitive people, readers may be inclined to join in poking fun at Jim. Yet, he represents a variety of viewpoints and may indeed be most representative of Twain's own ambivalence.

While he demonstrates throughout the novel that he has learned the important lesson of masking his feelings, of living behind the veil, Jim is also a manifestation of an acceptable character type for American readers. At the end of the novel when he could have saved himself from discovery, he comes out of hiding with the full knowledge that he is jeopardizing his freedom. Perhaps nowhere in American literature has the sacrificial nature of loyalty been more simply presented. Jim, however, is more than a shallow stereotype. When he first appears on Jackson's Island, he has outsmarted his owner who plans to sell him down the river for $800. His subsequent recitation of his wins and losses in speculative enterprises from banking to livestock—albeit elementary—lends credence to his final assertion that his riches now include himself and he is "wuth eight hund'd dollars." Early Jim and Huck establish a sense of trust, and the two runaways are mutually protective of each other despite Jim's legal impotence. Between them a form of racial integration takes place. While Huck lies to save Jim (and not without some misgivings), the older man is the instrument providing for Huck's "education." Whenever Huck is inclined to let the baseness of his human condition assume control, it is Jim who guides him. The bond between the two characters is so strong that if one takes Jim away, Huck—as we know him—ceases to exist.

Clearly, the relationship of Jim and Huck goes beyond that of a free white boy and an enslaved black man. Black mammies have become an integral part of American culture. There are still those who nostalgically recall childhood

---

BANNING *HUCKLEBERRY FINN*

Nat Hentoff is a literary critic and a best-selling author of young-adult literature. In the following excerpt of an article that he wrote for the Washington Post, *Hentoff discusses recent efforts by the National Association for the Advancement of Colored People (NAACP) to remove* Huckleberry Finn *from the reading lists of public schools, and recalls a discussion that he once had with a group of eighth-graders about the novel's racist content.*

The Pennsylvania State Conference of the NAACP has instructed its branches to file grievances with the state's human rights commission demanding that local school boards and district superintendents remove Mark Twain's "Adventures of Huckleberry Finn" from mandatory reading lists.

The charge, supported by the national NAACP, is that "tax dollars should not be used to perpetuate a stereotype that has psychologically damaging effects on the self-esteem of African American children."

Some years ago I was talking to African American eighth-graders in a Brooklyn public school who had been reading "Huckleberry Finn" in class—along with the history of racism in such towns as Hannibal, Missouri, where Twain had grown up.

The students recently had been discussing the passage in which Huck, on the raft with Jim, was tormented by what he had been raised to believe—that he would go to hell if he did not report this runaway slave to the owner.

Huck wrote a note doing just that, but finally, destroying the note, he said to himself, "All right, then, I'll *go* to hell!"

"Do you think we're so dumb," one of the Brooklyn eighth-graders said to me, "that we don't know the difference between a racist book and an anti-racist book? Sure, the book is full of the word 'Nigger.' That's how those bigots talked back then."

As Twain said years later, Huck, after writing the note, was struggling between "a sound heart" and "a deformed conscience" that he had to make right.

Nat Hentoff, "Expelling Huck Finn," *Washington Post*, November 27, 1999.

days with them. But little has been done with the black man in fiction. If he is not in the tradition of [Harriet Beecher Stowe's] Uncle Tom or [Joel Chandler Harris's] Uncle Remus, then he is often a fugitive from justice or from an enslaving society. While Jim is all of these, he is also the only "real" father that Huck has. We do not know much about Jim, but we do know that he has great love for his family and longs for the day when he will be free in order to reclaim them. In the meantime, Huck is his "family."

For most of the novel, one cannot forget that Huck—the free white boy—seems unusually preoccupied with matters of death. On the other hand, Jim—the enslaved black man—is concerned with life and manages to teach Huck something about the meaning of life itself. If Huck comes to demonstrate that conscience is not the captive of man-made laws or that it can transcend the restricting forces of society, Jim displays an affirmation of life that goes beyond the ignoble laws created to enslave. No matter how foolish Jim may appear and despite the number of times he is called "nigger," in the final analysis he cannot be burlesqued. But the fact that he is not absolutely part of that happy lot of plantation slaves [in] American literature is lost on those who reduce the novel to an exercise in name-calling.

Much has been written about Huck's so-called moral dilemma and crisis of conscience. Some readers get misty-eyed over the decision that the youngster must make without recognizing that Jim has also been forced to make choices. Of course, since it was against the law to help an escaping slave, Huck has to decide whether or not to commit a crime. Constitutional authorities might suggest that unjust laws must and can be changed only through an orderly process, but Huck is not enough in the mainstream to be privy to that process and consequently acts on instinct. Thus, one can argue that the novel is in reality the story of a boy who learns that the customs of his community really go counter to the best human interests. Needless to say, Huck does not rationalize this on a philosophical level. But, if Huck Finn with his questionable background, limited formal schooling, and restricted world can learn such a simple lesson, can not others learn it? Yet, what could have been a magnificent tale is so burdened by an excessive use of racial epithets that the story's message is lost to all but the most perceptive.

There is another ambiguity in the novel that not only relates to the nineteenth century but also—in a measure—speaks to the twentieth. If the color of one's skin is important (as some Americans believe), then readers need to look carefully at the description of Huck's father which contains a very specific reference to a white man: "There warn't no color in his face, where his face showed; it was white, not like another man's white, but a white to make a body sick, a white to make a body's flesh crawl—a tree-toad white, a fish-belly white." If one compares this description of Pap with that of the free black man from Ohio who so angered Huck's father that he refused to vote again or with the presentation of the noble qualities of Jim, "white" does not appear to have any particular advantage.

AMERICA'S AMBIVALENCE TOWARD RACIAL ISSUES

Later in the novel, in a very brief episode, Twain reveals another facet of American ambivalence toward racial issues. There is a tendency to accept blackness when it can be given a foreign air. In the day before public accommodation laws, some blacks pretended to be exotic foreigners in order to stay in hotels and eat in restaurants. It was a joke that delighted blacks and fooled whites. Twain's Duke and King are smart enough to know a dark-skinned foreigner is acceptable in the world of the Mississippi Valley. Thus, they dress Jim as a "Sick Arab." If he does not have to talk, then all of them are safe to travel on the raft during daylight hours.

Questioning the role of organized religion in race relations is as valid today as it was in the nineteenth century, despite the efforts of some churches to become "socially aware." The close relationship between American Christianity and slavery has not been overlooked by other studies. Twain, without belaboring the point, shows the commitment of Miss Watson, the Widow Douglas, and the Phelps family to the tenets of their church and their love of Bible-reading. If they find any incongruity between human slavery and what they profess to believe about religion, they keep it to themselves. To make certain that his readers understand that the church supports oppression, Twain—instead of pursuing the slavery/religion issue—introduces in the Grangerford incident a church which permits men to bring guns into the sanctuary. Clearly then, throughout the novel Twain shows organized religion to be faulty. The fact that Huck learns enough about its heaven and hell to realize that helping Jim will automatically consign him to the latter region is expressed in his famous declaration ("All right, then, I'll go to hell") even though his commitment to Jim is not complete enough for him to forget racial distinctions.

Some critics point with pride to Colonel Sherburn's famous speech against the cowardice of the mob. They claim that this is a clear example of Twain's intent. By dropping the voice of Huck, the novelist obviously makes that address stand out boldly. While aesthetically this shift in point of view may weaken the consistency of the work, Sherburn certainly makes a strong statement. But within the context of the novel, what does the Sherburn incident really mean? Noticeably, it does not alter the action except to save the Colonel from a mob although it does allow a brief platform for Twain to express his own contempt for mobs in an era known for such activities and lawlessness. However, if this mob is dispersed by the harsh reality of Sherburn's words, then the mob that recaptures Jim at the end of the novel is not concerned with the niceties of human behavior. If its members had not been aware that they could not pay for another's property or if the doctor had not requested that they "be no rougher than you're obleeged to," then this mob would not have been as yielding as the one which Sherburn faced.

An even more telling aspect of Twain's presentation of American race relations comes in the introduction of Tom's great escape plan for Jim at the end of the novel. The pragmatic Huck realizes the stupidity of their actions, as does Jim, but the romantic Tom insists they must follow him. In these episodic pranks, Jim is not only the victim but is also co-opted to go along in order to humor Tom who never considers that he is compromising the dignity of a man. Huck's silent assent to the procedure makes him an accessory. In the end, Tom does not succeed in freeing Jim, who is recaptured and faces the possibilities of even harsher treatment. The central irony should not escape the reader. While he has been in this final captivity, Jim has in reality been free—a fact that Tom suppresses in order to play his role and carry out his agenda. In the meantime, Jim's freedom has come from the old order: "Miss Watson died two months ago, and she was ashamed she ever was going to sell him down the river, and *said* so; and she set him free in her will."

Written during one of the darkest periods of American race relations, *Adventures of Huckleberry Finn* spoke to all segments of nineteenth-century society. Committed racists would have taken a perverse delight in the pseudo-minstrel antics of some of Jim's actions as well as the legitimizing of the word "nigger" by one of the nation's most popular writers. Those readers more inclined toward a sense of fairness would have been able to point with pride to the nobility of Jim or to his eventual freedom. They could take comfort in Colonel Sherburn's speech which, in a day of frequent lynchings, spoke to that brutality.

Present-day responses to the novel still probably operate on these two levels. While scholars may speak eloquently of the various themes to be found in Twain's work, to suggest the novel is a condemnation of the institution of slavery or that Jim represents the triumph of the human spirit over the most degrading attempts to subdue it might seem to be an optimistic begging of the question when others deplore the apparent elements of racism. That there is much concern with the presence of an objectionable word is perhaps unfortunate because to focus on an epithet seriously limits one's perception of other aspects of the novel. But such a concern is understandable and cannot be dismissed. It is also symptomatic of those latent attitudes that are so difficult to discard. Ultimately *Adventures of Huckleberry Finn* as a "classic" may tell more about the nation than many Americans want to know.

AN ENDURING MESSAGE

As an expression of the racial ambiguities of the United States, the novel goes beyond a catalogue of the ills of the nineteenth century. Although the days of physical slavery have passed, spiritual slavery continues supported by latter-day representatives of Miss Watson, Uncle Silas, and Aunt Sally. Meaning well, they continue to find solace and justifications for their actions within their religion. While the 1880s had a full share of racial romanticists who did not understand the reality of Reconstruction or the depth of feeling that was to mark the anti-black attitudes, modern America has not been free from equally unrealistic visions. Whether or not he intended to do so, Mark Twain unwittingly satirized those who would romanticize race problems and—in the process—prolong them. The romantic "do-gooders," like Tom, remain among us to conceive elaborate schemes that ultimately fail. Racial epithets are still—unfortunately—too much a part of the spoken and unspoken language of the nation. Notwithstanding desires to the contrary, for many Americans notions of superiority do not vary greatly from Pap's. They seldom stop to think of the illogical conclusions that result. It is "enough to make a body ashamed of the human race." On the other hand, the novel does suggest—and rightly so—that the fates and fortunes of the races are so closely intertwined that one cannot exist without the other. Either consciously or unconsciously, Twain produced a classic statement that weighs the nation in the balance. He described an America that was his and an America that is [ours]. To ban the novel is to condemn the messenger for the message.

Making Literary Humor a Respectable Profession

Alan Gribben

Alan Gribben credits Mark Twain with having an immeasurable overall effect on American literature, noting that his influence is evident in works ranging from such nineteenth-century writers as Stephen Crane and Hamlin Garland to the greatest writers of the twentieth century, including Ernest Hemingway, Sherwood Anderson, F. Scott Fitzgerald, and William Faulkner. Gribben argues that Mark Twain's innovative mixture of humor and serious subject matter enlightened publishers, reviewers, and readers alike on the possibilities of humor in literature, and that he is owed a debt of gratitude by his successors for having lent legitimacy and status to the genre of literary humor. Gribben asserts that Twain has yet to receive proper recognition for his works of literary criticism—works which he feels set the tone for present-day critical analysis of literary humor. Twain's literature continues to be viewed by academicians and ordinary readers alike as a reflection of the essence of America's national character and cultural heritage, and his humor is embraced as a grounding force in an era of overwhelming technological advances. Alan Gribben is Head of the Department of English and Philosophy at Auburn University in Montgomery, Alabama.

It is conceivable, if Samuel Clemens had somehow lived two decades longer, that he might have joined the set of writers associated with the *New Yorker* magazine—[Robert] Benchley, [E.B.] White, [Frank] Sullivan, [James] Thurber, John O'Hara, Dorothy Parker (and later, Corey Ford, S.J. Perelman, A.J. Liebling, and the others). Would Twain have be-

Excerpted from "The Importance of Mark Twain," by Alan Gribben, *American Quarterly*, vol. 37, no. 1 (1985), pp. 46–49; © The American Studies Association. Reprinted by permission of the Johns Hopkins University Press. Footnotes in the original have been omitted in this reprint.

come a revered member of the Algonquin Hotel crowd, slicing away with scalpel-like wit while seated with George Kaufman at the famous Round Table? Would he have appeared in the pages of the same magazine that today carries Woody Allen's casuals? Quite likely, for Mark Twain was ever alert to the winds of comedic change. Mark Twain became, after all, "Mark Twain"; his legend grew, at his encouragement, and he grew along with it as man and writer. It is exceedingly difficult to live within the confines of expectations harbored by one's public; stage and screen personalities and even novelists like Kurt Vonnegut, Jr., and Norman Mailer, whose private lives are spotlighted relentlessly, can tire of their own aura. Yet Clemens adapted to this excruciating role, thrived in it, and died in the process of adding new dimensions to it. This is an astounding achievement, one that has not yet been adequately appreciated by his biographers. The early hunger for renown by a river-village youth cannot account for the energy that the mature Clemens lavished in shoring up his public image; it is easy to understand why so many sentimental commentators have gushed about the "original" character whom he left behind for future ages. As his image came into focus, Mark Twain knew by instinct what Americans wanted and needed in the way of mythic figures, and he provided one that will evidently last as long as our country. No one else had the diplomacy, talent, audacity, or the desire requisite to leave behind that majestic, white-maned, ingratiating image in our collective mind. For most students and many teachers, Mark Twain embodies what is memorable and noteworthy about the post–Civil War decades of literary realism and our national experience.

FORERUNNER OF AMERICAN LITERARY REALISM

Thinking about Twain's importance to American literature and humor, one finds it almost impossible to disagree with commonplaces of literary history that seem in little danger of being overturned. Mark Twain *did* signal the end of the American Romantic era, as survey works and textbooks announce routinely. Although Mark Twain's collected literary criticism has yet to appear as a volume in the Mark Twain Papers Series, a few of his animadversions against Jane Austen, Sir Walter Scott, George Meredith, and others have made known his jocular attitude about critical principles and his devotion to realistic precepts of his own time. Unfairly but magnificently malicious, and as famous as Hemingway's eulogy to *Huckleberry Finn* in *Green Hills of Africa,* Twain's "Fenimore Cooper's Literary Offences" has become a staple of anthologies and actually helps students sense the buried resentment against preceding Romantic writers that partially motivated Twain and other realist authors. In pieces like this one and in the marginalia in his copies of Bret Harte's works ("One of those brutal California stage-drivers could not be polite to a passenger,—& not one of the guild ever 'sir'd' *anybody,*" he groused), Twain revealed himself as a close observer of detail, nuance, and diction—opening the way for less stuffy approaches to essays in literary criticism. He is undoubtedly one of the chief inspirations for the small but welcome band of academic wits—among them, Hamlin Hill, James M. Cox, John Gerber, Jesse Bier, Louis D. Rubin, Jr., Leslie Fiedler, and John Seelye—who in the 1970s and 1980s could be entertaining in their own right when reading conference papers or writing reviews and articles about American humor. Mark Twain's tone enabled them to realize that unbroken solemnity in discussing humor is simply asking for a pie in the face, or is at least inviting another Woody Allen lampoon in the *New Yorker* about the hilarious obtuseness of pompous professors.

Mark Twain's aggregate influence is immeasurable, but we know at least that his books appeared on the library shelves of some the most talented younger writers of his period—Stephen Crane and Hamlin Garland, for instance. [Literary critic] Jay Hubbell notes that Twain's influence on writers of fiction "is greater than that of any other American writer except Henry James." Scholars have discerned the impact of Mark Twain on the works of Ernest Hemingway, Sherwood Anderson, Thomas Wolfe, F. Scott Fitzgerald, and William Faulkner.

A Touchstone of Cultural Heritage

If Mark Twain had never existed, if young Sam Clemens had succumbed to an early illness, as his family expected, or had he drowned in the Mississippi River, like several of his boyhood chums, then something in our literature would be tangibly missing, and we would know it. What we professors and students and readers would find lacking would be our linkage point with the nineteenth century, especially with its humor, in the form of an actual man whom we can admire and feel affection toward. Mark Twain is one of our few symbolic means of maintaining the crucial continuity between our past cultural heritage and our present-day attitudes. He is a reference figure for all of us, citizen-readers and artist-comedians, marking the common denominator of what we want to perceive to be the American character. As a public speaker and lecturer, indeed, Mark Twain was very possibly our last performing humorist who presented himself as a "general" personage—neither an easterner nor exactly a westerner, the embodiment instead of the entire sum of national regionalism, all parts equal, none predominating. This "generic" persona, so different from [cowboy philosopher] Will Rogers's lariat-twirling actor, is equally remote from the ethnic *shtick* of Woody Allen and Richard Pryor or the urban neurosis of Joan Rivers and David Brenner. He has no direct, obvious successors, only his impersonators; the humor of our contemporary nightclubs is fragmented and typecast. The foe of humbug, explicitly rebelling against outworn Romantic forms and themes, he detested high airs and smug complacency—putting him in the progression that has led to the stand-up insults of W.C. Fields as well as Lenny Bruce.

Learning from [Southwestern humorist] Artemus Ward and others, Twain mastered discriminative lessons of theatricality and publicity. Among other feats, he contrived his public persona so as to convey the impression of (feigned) laziness, lack of erudition, easy success. If the current generation of nonreading Americans is less familiar than their literate predecessors with the qualities of his lesser works, and sometimes even with his greatest novels, at least he is often quoted from pulpits, in newspaper columns, and at lecterns. He has gained favor with academicians while retaining his hold on the taste of the ordinary reader, something that Poe's fiction accomplished but O. Henry's failed to bring off.

RAISING THE BAR OF LITERARY HUMOR

Mark Twain endures because he is greater than any of his possible classifications—crackerbarrel philosopher, literary comedian, world traveler, realist, Naturalist, hoaxer, novelist, vernacular humorist, after-dinner speaker—with which he might be labeled. He did practically everything that was expected of a man of letters in his age, and he generally acquitted himself well in every department. He gave his countrymen pride in themselves, their humor, their literature. And he elevated the station of his calling: among Twain's achievements, one of his grandest was his success in making literary humor seem like a respectable profession. His wealth, his Nook Farm home, his fraternal relations with the influential and the lionized—these and other signs of status laid a benediction on his career so lasting that all subsequent authors of comic sketches, stories, and novels owe him a large debt. He rescued the funnyman from the smudged-print pages of [Josh] Billings, [John] Phoenix, and [Petroleum V.] Nasby and restored him to the honored tradition of Benjamin Franklin, Oliver Wendell Holmes, and James Russell Lowell. Moreover, Twain mixed seriousness and comedy so subtly in works like *A Connecticut Yankee in King Arthur's Court* that he himself did not always understand his initial intentions, and he thus educated publishers and reviewers and readers about the deeper possibilities of humor, preparing American audiences for John Cheever, Kurt Vonnegut, Jr., Thomas Berger, John Barth, and others.

American literature would have flourished without Mark Twain's contributions. Yet it would be stuffier, less colorful, less redolent of the river and the West, less alluring. He has given us, along with rich impressions of life on rafts, steamboats, stage coaches, railroad cars, and ocean ships, a reassurance that we are not traveling into some black hole of the future, that we have a renewable and accessible past that guarantees a sane and attainable future. By finding amusement in the writings and speeches of one American figure of the nineteenth century, we assuage disturbing anxieties about our historical and cultural isolation when we contemplate with misgivings the dawning age of computer technology, biological engineering, and galactic transportation. If we can palpably touch the steamboat pilot's wheel with Mark Twain, then our grip on the spaceship controls of the twenty-first century feels surer as we extend our capacity to shuttle a supply of humor into the farther reaches of human history.

Discussion Questions

Chapter 1

1. Consider the less-pleasant aspects of Mark Twain's childhood, as discussed in John Lauber's essay "Mark Twain's Childhood." How did these experiences serve to shape Mark Twain's personality as an adult?

2. How, according to James M. Cox, did Mark Twain's experiences in the Nevada Territory allow for the discovery of his literary persona?

3. Ron Powers suggests that Mark Twain's views on life underwent significant changes as a result of his brief career as a riverboat pilot. Do such changes seem to be a likely outcome of Twain's piloting experiences? Why?

Chapter 2

1. Do you agree with Don Florence's assertion that it is a self-defeating enterprise for readers to try to identify and analyze the influence of Samuel Clemens on the literary works of Mark Twain? Why?

Chapter 3

1. William Baker suggests that Mark Twain's success in the realm of literary humor hinged on his masterful application of three specific literary techniques in his works. Do you think that Mark Twain's distinction as a humorist can be fairly reduced to his mastery of these three techniques?

2. Shelley Fisher Fishkin discusses Mark Twain's forging of a literature that was uniquely American in spirit rather than an imitation of British or European literature. What value would such a literary innovation have been to the nation?

3. Eric Mottram notes that Mark Twain's humor would transition into the realm of cynical political satire as his career evolved. What benefit or harm might such works of satire be to society?

CHAPTER 4

1. Name some of the places where you have seen Mark Twain's image in society. What connotations does his image evoke for you, your parents, and your grandparents?

2. Alan Gribben suggests that Mark Twain's literature is still of tremendous relevance to modern-day American society. Do you agree with this assessment of his work? Explain.

3. Kenny J. Williams notes that efforts to ban *The Adventures of Huckleberry Finn* from public schools and libraries are constantly underway and are based primarily on the novel's use of racial epithets. Is this sufficient reason for this or any novel to be banned? If not, under what circumstances, if any, should a novel be banned?

Appendix of Documents

Document 1: Henry Clemens' Death

The summer of 1858 would bring one of the many tragedies that Mark Twain would endure during the course of his life when his younger brother, Henry, succumbed to injuries sustained in an explosion aboard the steamboat on which he had been employed. Having also worked on the steamboat until just prior to the explosion, Twain had gotten Henry his job, and would suffer a lifetime of guilt on account of Henry's death. The following is an excerpt of a letter written by Twain on June 18th, 1858, in which he informs his sister-in-law of Henry's death and expresses the immensity of his grief and guilt.

Dear Sister Mollie:

Long before this reaches you, my poor Henry,—my darling, my pride, my glory, my *all*, will have finished his blameless career, and the light of my life will have gone out in utter darkness. O, God! this is hard to bear. Hardened, hopeless,—aye, lost—lost—lost and ruined sinner as I am—I, even *I*, have humbled myself to the ground and prayed as never man prayed before, that the great God might let this cup pass from me—that he would strike me to the earth, but spare my brother—that he would pour out the fulness of his just wrath upon my wicked head, but have mercy, mercy, mercy upon that unoffending boy. The horrors of three days have swept over me—they have blasted my youth and left me an old man before my time. Mollie, there are grey hairs in my head to-night. For forty-eight hours I labored at the bedside of my poor burned and bruised, but uncomplaining brother, and then the star of my hope went out and left me in the gloom of despair. Then poor wretched me, that was once so proud, was humbled to the very dust—lower than the dust—for the vilest beggar in the streets of Saint Louis could never conceive of a humiliation like mine. Men take me by the hand and *congratulate* me, and call me "lucky" because I was not on the Pennsylvania when she blew up! My God forgive them, for they know not what they say.

Edgar Marquess Branch, Michael B. Frank and Kenneth M. Sanderson, eds., *Mark Twain's Letters, Volume I, 1853–1866.* Los Angeles: University of California Press, 1988, pp. 80–81.

DOCUMENT 2: A CALL TO LITERATURE

In 1865, as Mark Twain's unique journalism quickly and unexpect-edly began to receive national acclaim, he began to sense the enor-mity of his potential as a Western humorist. The following is an ex-cerpt of a letter he sent to his brother Orion, in which he explains that, though he finds humorous literature base, he feels that God has imbued him with a special gift for writing such material, and that it is therefore his duty to do so.

I never had but two **powerful** ambitions in my life. One was to be a pilot, & the other a preacher of the gospel. I accomplished the one & failed in the other, **because** I could not supply myself with the necessary stock in trade—*i.e.* religion. I have given it up forever. I never had a "call" in that direction, anyhow, & my aspirations were the very ecstasy of presumption. But I *have* had a "call" to litera-ture, of a low order—*i.e.* humorous. It is nothing to be proud of, but it is my strongest suit, & if I were to listen to that maxim of stern *duty* which says that to do right you must multiply the one or the two or the three talents which the Almighty entrusts to your keep-ing, I would long ago have ceased to meddle with things for which I was by nature unfitted & turned my attention to seriously scrib-bling to excite the laughter of God's creatures. Poor, pitiful busi-ness! Though the Almighty did His part by me—for the talent is a mighty engine when supplied with the steam of education—which I have not got, & so its pistons & cylinders & shafts move feebly & for a holiday show & are useless for any good purpose.

Edgar Marquess Branch, Michael B. Frank and Kenneth M. Sanderson, eds., *Mark Twain's Letters, Volume I, 1853–1866.* Berkeley: University of California Press, 1988, pp. 322–23.

DOCUMENT 3: EARLY SOCIAL CRITICISM

As a journalist in the Nevada Territory and in San Francisco be-tween 1862 and 1866, Mark Twain would frequently find himself in trouble with prominent local officials over the scathing and ac-cusatory satirical pieces that he had written about them. The fol-lowing is an excerpt of one such piece, in which he criticizes the chief of the San Francisco Police Department.

I want to compliment Chief Burke—I do honestly. But I can't find anything to compliment him about. He is always rushing furiously around, like a dog after his own tail—and with the same general re-sult, it seems to me; if he catches it, it don't amount to anything, af-ter all the fuss; and if he don't t catch it it don't make any difference, because he didn't want it anyhow; he only wanted the exercise, and the happiness of "showing off" before his mistress and the other young ladies. But if the Chief would only do something praisewor-thy, I would be the first and the most earnest and cordial to give him the credit due. I would sling him a compliment that would knock him down. I mean that it would be such a first-class compliment that it might surprise him to that extent as coming from me.

Gary Scharnhorst, "Mark Twain's Imbroglio with the San Francisco Police: Three Lost Texts," *American Literature*, vol. 62, no. 4, December 1990, pp. 687–88.

DOCUMENT 4: THE SANDWICH ISLANDS LECTURE

The following is an excerpt of the Sandwich Islands lecture that Mark Twain delivered in San Francisco on October 2, 1866. In this, his first-ever professional lecture, one finds the frequent, humorous digressions from the topic at hand that would come to characterize Twain's lectures and literature.

Ladies and gentlemen: The next lecture in this course will be delivered this evening, by Samuel L. Clemens, a gentleman whose high character and unimpeachable integrity are only equalled by his comeliness of person and grace of manner. And I am the man! I was obliged to excuse the chairman from introducing me, because he never compliments anybody and I knew I could do it just as well.

The Sandwich Islands will be the subject of my lecture—when I get to it—and I shall endeavor to tell the truth as nearly as a newspaper man can. If I embellish it with a little nonsense, that makes no difference; it won't mar the truth; it is only as the barnacle ornaments the oyster by sticking to it. That figure is original with me! I was born back from tidewater and don't know as the barnacle *does* stick to the oyster.

Unfortunately, the first object I ever saw in the Sandwich Islands was a repulsive one. It was a case of Oriental leprosy, of so dreadful a nature that I have never been able to get it out of my mind since. I don't intend that it shall give a disagreeable complexion to this lecture at all, but inasmuch as it was the first thing I saw in those islands, it naturally suggested itself when I proposed to talk about the islands. It is a very hard matter to get a disagreeable object out of one's memory. I discovered that a good while ago. When I made that funeral excursion in the *Quaker City* they showed me some very interesting objects in a cathedral, and I expected to recollect every one of them—but I didn't. I forgot every one of them—except one—and that I remembered because it was unpleasant. It was a curious piece of ancient sculpture. They don't know where they got it nor how long they have had it. It is a stone figure of a man without any skin—a freshly skinned man showing every vein, artery and tissue. It was the heaviest thing, and yet there was something fascinating about it. It looked so natural; it looked as if it was in pain, and you know a freshly skinned man would naturally look that way. He would unless his attention was occupied with some other matter. It was a dreadful object, and I have been sorry many a time since that I ever saw that man. Sometimes I dream of him, sometimes he is standing by my bedpost, sometimes he is stretched between the sheets, touching me—the most uncomfortable bedfellow I ever had.

I can't get rid of unpleasant recollections. Once when I ran away from school I was afraid to go home at night, so I crawled through a window and laid down on a lounge in my father's office. The moon shed a ghastly light in the room, and presently I descried a long, dark mysterious shape on the floor. I wanted to go and touch it—but I didn't—I restrained myself—I didn't do it. I had a good deal of presence of mind—tried to go to sleep—kept thinking of it. By and by when the moonlight fell upon it, I saw that it was a dead man lying there with his white face turned up in the moonlight. I never was so sick in all my life. I never wanted to take a walk so bad! I went away from there. I didn't hurry—simply went out of the window—and took the sash along with me. I didn't need the sash, but it was handier to take it than to leave it. I wasn't scared, but I was a good deal agitated. I have never forgotten that man. He had fallen dead in the street and they brought him in there to try him, and they brought him in guilty, too.

But I am losing time; what I have been saying don't bear strictly on the Sandwich Islands, but one reminiscence leads to another, and I am obliged to bring myself down in this way, on account of that unpleasant thing that I first saw there.

Paul Fatout, ed., *Mark Twain Speaking.* Iowa City: University of Iowa Press, 1976, pp. 4–5.

DOCUMENT 5: ROUGHING IT

As a gold and silver miner in the Nevada Territory during 1861–1862, Mark Twain would encounter countless men who, like himself, had been infected with that peculiar form of optimism known to locals as "miner's fever." In the following passage from Roughing It, *Mark Twain recalls one of the ways that these miners attempted to keep themselves fed as they sought their fortunes in the dirt.*

I met men at every turn who owned from one thousand to thirty thousand "feet" in undeveloped silver mines, every single foot of which they believed would shortly be worth from fifty to a thousand dollars—and as often as any other way they were men who had not twenty-five dollars in the world. Every man you met had his new mine to boast of, and his "specimens" ready; and if the opportunity offered, he would infallibly back you into a corner and offer as a favor to *you,* not to *him,* to part with just a few feet in the "Golden Age," or the "Sarah Jane," or some other unknown stack of croppings, for money enough to get a "square meal" with, as the phrase went. And you were never to reveal that he had made you the offer at such a ruinous price, for it was only out of friendship for you that he was willing to make the sacrifice. Then he would fish a piece of rock out of his pocket, and after looking mysteriously around as if he feared he might be waylaid and robbed if caught with such wealth in his possession, he would dab the rock against his tongue, clap an eye-glass to it, and exclaim:

"Look at that! Right there in that red dirt! See it? See the specks of gold? And the streak of silver? That's from the 'Uncle Abe.' There's a hundred thousand tons like that in sight! Right in sight, mind you! And when we get down on it and the ledge comes in solid, it will be the richest thing in the world! Look at the assay! I don't want you to believe *me*—look at the assay!"

Then he would get out a greasy sheet of paper which showed that the portion of rock assayed had given evidence of containing silver and gold in the proportion of so many hundreds or thousands of dollars to the ton. I little knew, then, that the custom was to hunt out the *richest* piece of rock and get it assayed!

Mark Twain, *Roughing It.* Berkeley: University of California Press, 1993, p. 195.

DOCUMENT 6: MARK TWAIN'S FAUX PAS

On December 17, 1877, Mark Twain would give a speech for the revered American writers Ralph Waldo Emerson, Henry Longfellow, and Oliver Wendell Holmes. Told with a thick, Western drawl, the speech was intended to be a harmless, witty yarn about a miner that he had met in the West who had been duped the previous day by three men claiming to have been Emerson, Longfellow, and Holmes. Though Twain had been unaware beforehand of the underlying sentiments that had prompted the story he told, the audience's cool response revealed the speech's subtext to him: The works of these three American writers were largely imitative of those of Britain and Europe, and as such, these men were impostors. The following is an excerpt from that speech.

"As I said, Mr. Twain, you are the fourth in twenty-four hours—and I'm a-going to move—I ain't suited to a littery atmosphere."

I said to the miner, "Why, my dear sir, *these* were not the gracious singers to whom we and the world pay loving reverence and homage; these were imposters."

The miner investigated me with a calm eye for a while, then said he, "Ah—imposters, were they?—are *you?*" I did not pursue the subject; and since then I haven't traveled on my *nom de plume* enough to hurt. Such is the reminiscence I was moved to contribute, Mr. Chairman. In my enthusiasm I may have exaggerated the details a little, but you will easily forgive me that fault, since I believe it is the first time I have ever deflected from perpendicular fact on an occasion like this.

Paul Fatout, ed., *Mark Twain Speaking.* Iowa City: University of Iowa Press, 1976, p. 114.

DOCUMENT 7: MARK TWAIN'S FAUX PAS

Mark Twain's inadvertent derision of Ralph Waldo Emerson, Henry Longfellow, and Oliver Wendell Holmes during the speech that he gave for them on December 17, 1877, was perhaps more of a shock to himself than any other person in attendance. The following is an apology letter that he would write to the three men on December 27, 1877.

To Mr. Emerson, Mr. Longfellow, & Dr. Holmes:

Gentlemen: I come before you, now, with the mien & posture of the guilty—not to excuse, gloss, or extenuate, but only to offer my repentance. If a man with a fine nature had done that thing which I did, it would have been a crime—because all his senses would have warned him against it beforehand; but I did it innocently & unwarned. I did it as innocently as I ever did anything. . . . But when I perceived what it was that I had done, I felt as real a sorrow & suffered as sharp a mortification as if I had done it with a guilty intent. This continues. That the impulse was innocent, brings no abatement. As to my wife's distress, it is not to be measured; for she is of finer stuff than I; & yours were sacred names to her. We do not talk about this misfortune—it *scorches;* so we only think—and think.

I will end, now. I *had* to write you, for the easement of it, even though the doing it might maybe be a further offense. "But I do not ask you to forgive what I did that night, for it is not forgivable; I simply had it at heart to ask you to believe that I am only heedlessly a savage, not premeditatedly; & that I am under as severe punishment as even you could adjudge to me if you were required to appoint my penalty. I do not ask you to say one word in answer to this; it is not needful, & would of course be distasteful & difficult. I beg you to consider that in letting me unbosom myself you will do me an act of grace that will be sufficient in itself. I wanted to write such a letter as this, that next morning in Boston, but one of wiser judgment advised against it, & said Wait.

With great & sincere respect

I am

Truly Yours

Saml. L. Clemens

Paul Fatout, ed., *Mark Twain Speaking*. Iowa City: University of Iowa Press, 1976, pp. 177–78.

Document 8: Huckleberry Finn's Decision

Throughout Mark Twain's childhood in Hannibal, Missouri, he was taught that the institution of slavery was advocated by God in the Bible, and that it was a sin for one to help a slave escape to freedom. In Adventures of Huckleberry Finn, *young Huck is confused by the contradictions between that which he has been taught regarding slavery, and that which his heart tells him to do about his river-rafting companion, Jim, who is a runaway slave. In an effort to save his soul, Huck has gone so far as to write an anonymous letter to Jim's master informing her of Jim's whereabouts, but begins to have second thoughts about delivering the letter. Never presuming to question the accuracy of what he has been taught on the matter of slavery, Huck must thus choose between eternal damnation and the*

*betrayal of a friend. In the following passage, Huck comes to a deci-
sion on the matter.*

I felt good and all washed clean of sin for the first time I had ever
felt so in my life, and I knowed I could pray, now. But I didn't do it
straight off, but laid the paper down and set there thinking; thinking how good it was all this happened so, and how near I come to
being lost and going to hell. And went on thinking. And got to
thinking over our trip down the river; and I see Jim before me, all
the time, in the day, and in the night-time, sometimes moonlight,
sometimes storms, and we a floating along, talking, and singing,
and laughing. But somehow I couldn't seem to strike no places to
harden me against him, but only the other kind. I'd see him standing my watch on top of his'n, stead of calling me—so I could go on
sleeping; and see him how glad he was when I come back out of
the fog; and when I come to him again in the swamp, up there
where the feud was; and such-like times; and would always call me
honey, and pet me, and do everything he could think of for me, and
how good he always was; and at last I struck the time I saved him
by telling the men we had small-pox aboard, and he was so grate-
ful, and said I was the best friend old Jim ever had in the world, and
the *only* one he's got now; and then I happened to look around, and
see that paper.

It was a close place. I took it up, and held it in my hand. I was a
trembling, because I'd got to decide, forever, betwixt two things,
and I knowed it. I studied a minute, sort of holding my breath, and
then says to myself:

"All right then, I'll *go* to hell"—and tore it up.

It was awful thoughts, and awful words, but they was said. And
I let them stay said; and never thought no more about reforming. I
shoved the whole thing out of my head; and said I would take up
wickedness again, which was in my line, being brung up to it, and
the other warn't. And for a starter, I would go to work and steal Jim
out of slavery again; and if I could think up anything worse, I would
do that, too; because as long as I was in, and in for good, I might as
well go the whole hog.

Mark Twain, *Adventures of Huckleberry Finn.* Berkeley: University of California Press,
1986, pp. 268–71.

DOCUMENT 9: MARK TWAIN ON BANNING *HUCKLEBERRY FINN*

*Mark Twain frequently corresponded with readers who had written
him to comment on* Adventures of Huckleberry Finn, *and in 1905
he received such a letter from a librarian at Brooklyn Public Library.
The librarian, who was opposing a fellow librarian's crusade to
have the novel removed from the children's section of the library,
had sought Twain's advice on how best to proceed. This is Mark
Twain's tongue-in-cheek response to the librarian's plea for guid-*

ance, in which he claims to endorse the effort to remove the novel from the children's section.

November 21, 1905

Dear Sir:

I am greatly troubled by what you say. I wrote Tom Sawyer and Huck Finn for adults exclusively, and it always distresses me when I find that boys and girls have been allowed access to them. The mind that becomes soiled in youth can never again be washed clean; I know this by my own experience, and to this day I cherish an unappeasable bitterness against the unfaithful guardians of my young life, who not only permitted but compelled me to read an un-expurgated Bible through before I was 15 years old. None can do that and ever draw a clean sweet breath again this side of the grave. Ask that young lady—she will tell you so.

Most honestly do I wish I could say a softening word or two in defence of Huck's character, since you wish it, but really in my opinion it is no better than those of Solomon, David, Satan, and the rest of the sacred brotherhood.

If there is an unexpurgated in the Children's Department, won't you please help that young woman remove Huck and Tom from that questionable companionship?

Sincerely yours,

S.L. CLEMENS.

"Bantering With A Brooklyn Librarian," *Humanities*, January/February 2000, vol. 21, issue 1, p. 12.

DOCUMENT 10: MARK TWAIN ON WESTERN IMPERIALISM

Between 1895 and 1900, while on a round-the-world lecturing tour, Mark Twain would witness firsthand the fruits of American and European imperialism in the world. In the following two sentences, which appeared in the New York Herald *on December 30, 1900, Twain sums up his views on what he had seen abroad.*

I bring you the stately matron named Christendom, returning bedraggled, besmirched and dishonored from pirate-raids in Kiao-Chou, Manchuria, South Africa & the Philippines, with her soul full of meanness, her pocket full of boodle and her mouth full of pious hypocrisies. Give her the soap and a towel, but hide the looking-glass.

Mark Twain, "A Greeting from the Nineteenth Century to the Twentieth Century," printed in Hamlin Hill, *Mark Twain: God's Fool.* New York: Harper & Row, 1973.

DOCUMENT 11: UNEARTHING MARK TWAIN'S TRUTH

In the following excerpt from Mark Twain's Autobiography, *Mark Twain notes that the audience may not have believed much of the speech that he had given at his recent 70th birthday party, and discusses his lifelong gift for embellishing the truth.*

In the birthday speech which I made were concealed many facts. I expected everybody to discount those facts 95 per cent, and that is probably what happened. That does not trouble me; I am used to having my statements discounted. My mother had begun it before I was seven years old. But all through my life my facts have had a substratum of truth, and therefore they were not without value. Any person who is familiar with me knows how to strike my average, and therefore knows how to get at the jewel of any fact of mine and dig it out of its blue-clay matrix. My mother knew that art. When I was seven or eight or ten or twelve years old—along there—a neighbor said to her, "Do you ever believe anything that that boy says?" My mother said, "He is the wellspring of truth, but you can't bring up the whole well with one bucket"—and she added, "I know his average, therefore he never deceives me. I discount him 90 per cent for embroidery, and what is left is perfect and priceless truth, without a flaw in it anywhere."

Samuel Clemens, *Mark Twain's Autobiography.* New York: Harper & Brothers, 1924, pp. 293–94.

DOCUMENT 12: PAINE DEFENDS MARK TWAIN'S POSTHUMOUS IMAGE

A full sixteen years after Mark Twain's death, his official biographer, Albert Bigelow Paine, still felt that he had both a personal and professional stake in the preservation of the image of Mark Twain that was portrayed in Mark Twain's Autobiography. *In the following excerpt of a letter written in 1926 by Paine to the book's publisher, Harper & Brothers, he encourages the company to continue to take legal efforts to prevent the publication of any other books about Mark Twain.*

I think on general principles it is a mistake to let any one else write about Mark Twain, as long as we ran prevent it. . . . As soon as this is begun (writing about him at all, I mean) the Mark Twain that we have "preserved"—the Mark Twain that we knew, the traditional Mark Twain—will begin to fade and change, and with that process the Harper Mark Twain property will depreciate.

Excerpted in Hamlin Hill, *Mark Twain: God's Fool.* New York: Harper & Row, 1973, p. 268.

CHRONOLOGY

1835

Samuel Langhorne Clemens is born to John and Jane Clemens on November 30 in Florida, Missouri.

1839

The Clemens family moves to Hannibal, Missouri.

1847

Clemens's father, John Marshall Clemens, dies of pneumonia on March 24.

1848

Clemens is apprenticed to printer Joseph P. Ament of the Hannibal *Gazette*.

1849

Clemens's first published work—a humorous piece to which he signed the pseudonym "Devil"—appears in the Hannibal *Western Union* on November 14.

1853

Clemens completes his apprenticeship, serves for three years as a journeyman printer in St. Louis, New York, Philadelphia, and then again in New York; some of his letters home are published in the Hannibal *Journal*.

1857

Clemens becomes apprentice ("cub") Mississippi River steamboat pilot under Horace Bixby.

1858

Clemens becomes a licensed steamboat pilot.

1861

The Civil War brings steamboating on the Mississippi to a halt in May; in June, Clemens serves briefly in a volunteer Confederate battalion; in August, he and brother Orion arrive in the Nevada Territory; Sam spends the duration of the year prospecting for silver and gold.

1862

Clemens has "Josh" letters published in the Virginia City *Territorial Enterprise* between February and July; in September, Clemens becomes a reporter for the *Territorial Enterprise* at Virginia City.

1863

On February 2 Clemens first uses the pseudonym "Mark Twain" in a humorous piece for the *Territorial Enterprise.*

1864

Twain arrives in San Francisco on May 29 and obtains employment with the *Morning Call.*

1866

Twain spends four months in the Sandwich Islands (Hawaii) as a correspondent for the Sacramento *Daily Union* and embarks on a tour giving lectures about the experience upon his return to San Francisco.

1867

The Celebrated Jumping Frog of Calaveras County and Other Sketches is published on May 1; in June, Twain departs on the *Quaker City* for a tour of the Mediterranean and the Holy Land as a correspondent for the San Francisco *Alta California;* on December 27 Twain meets Olivia "Livy" Langdon for the first time.

1868

The Innocents Abroad is published.

1870

Twain marries Olivia Langdon on February 2; on November 7 Langdon Clemens, son of Twain and Olivia, is born.

1872

Roughing It is published in February; on March 19 Olivia Susan "Susy" Clemens is born at Elmira; on June 2 Langdon Clemens dies; on July 15 Twain begins writing *Tom Sawyer,* which he intends to be a play.

1873

A collaboration between Twain and Charles Dudley Warner, entitled *The Gilded Age,* is published in December.

1874

Clara Clemens is born on June 8.

1875

Sketches New and Old is published.

1876

The Adventures of Tom Sawyer is published on June 9; in July, Mark Twain begins writing *The Adventures of Huckleberry Finn.*

1879

A Tramp Abroad is published on March 13.

1880

Jean Clemens is born on July 26.

1882

Life on the Mississippi is published on May 12; in December, *The Prince and the Pauper* is published.

1885

The Adventures of Huckleberry Finn is published.

1889

A Connecticut Yankee in King Arthur's Court is published.

1891

The Paige typesetting machine, an invention that Mark Twain had backed with $190,000, proved to be a failure.

1892

The American Claimant is published in May.

1893

In July, *Mark Twain: The Story of His Life and Work* by Will M. Clemens is published by the Clemens Publishing Company.

1894

Pudd'nhead Wilson is published in May.

1895

Twain embarks on a round-the-world lecturing tour to recover his devastated finances.

1896

Joan of Arc is published in May; on August 18 Susy Clemens dies at Hartford of meningitis while Twain is in England.

1897

Following the Equator is published on November 13.

1900

The Man That Corrupted Hadleyburg is published on June 11.

1904

Extracts from Adam's Diary is published on April 6; on June 5 Olivia Clemens dies in Florence, Italy.

1906

On January 9 Mark Twain began dictating his life story, which was made into a biography by Albert Bigelow Paine.

1907

Oxford University confers on Mark Twain the degree of doctor of literature on June 26.

1909

Jean Clemens dies on December 24.

1910

Twain suffers severe pains of angina and goes to Bermuda from early January until early April in an effort to recover his health; on April 21 Twain dies at his home in Connecticut; on April 24 Twain is buried beside his wife, Olivia, daughters Jean and Susy, and son, Langdon, in Woodlawn Cemetery in Elmira, New York.

1912

Mark Twain's Autobiography is published.

FOR FURTHER RESEARCH

BOOKS AND OTHER WRITINGS BY MARK TWAIN

Samuel Clemens, *Mark Twain's Autobiography*. New York: Harper & Brothers, 1924.

The Adventures of Huckleberry Finn. New York: Oxford University Press, 1996.

The Adventures of Tom Sawyer. New York: Oxford University Press, 1996.

The Celebrated Jumping Frog of Calaveras County and Other Sketches. New York: Oxford University Press, 1996.

A Connecticut Yankee in King Arthur's Court. New York: Oxford University Press, 1996.

Extracts from Adam's Diary. New York: Oxford University Press, 1996.

Following the Equator. New York: Oxford University Press, 1996.

The Innocents Abroad. New York: Oxford University Press, 1996.

Life on the Mississippi. New York: Oxford University Press, 1996.

The Man That Corrupted Hadleyburg. New York: Oxford University Press, 1996.

Mark My Words: Mark Twain on Writing. Ed. Mark Dawidziak. New York: St. Martin's Press, 1996.

Mark Twain Speaks for Himself. Ed. Paul Fatout. West Lafayette, IN: Purdue University Press, 1978.

Mark Twain's Letters to His Publishers. Ed. Hamlin Hill. Berkeley and Los Angeles: University of California Press, 1967.

The Prince and the Pauper. New York: Oxford University Press, 1996.

Pudd'nhead Wilson. New York: Oxford University Press, 1996.

Roughing It. New York: Oxford University Press, 1996.

Sketches New and Old. New York: Oxford University Press, 1996.

A Tramp Abroad. New York: Oxford University Press, 1996.

When in Doubt, Tell the Truth and Other Quotations from Mark Twain. Ed. Brian Collins. New York: Columbia University Press, 1996.

Mark Twain and Charles Dudley Warner, *The Gilded Age.* New York: Oxford University Press, 1996.

BIOGRAPHIES AND STUDIES OF MARK TWAIN

Jonathan Arac, *Huckleberry Finn as Idol and Target: The Functions of Criticism in Our Time.* Madison: University of Wisconsin Press, 1997.

Louis J. Budd, *Our Mark Twain: The Making of His Public Personality.* Philadelphia: University of Pennsylvania Press, 1983.

Guy Cardwell, *The Man Who Was Mark Twain: Images and Ideologies.* New Haven, CT: Yale University Press, 1991.

Jocelyn Chadwick-Joshua, *The Jim Dilemma: Reading Race in Huckleberry Finn.* Oxford: University Press of Mississippi, 1998.

James M. Cox, *Mark Twain: The Fate of Humor.* Princeton, NJ: University Press, 1996.

Everett Emerson, *The Authentic Mark Twain: A Literary Biography of Samuel Clemens.* Philadelphia: University of Pennsylvania Press, 1984.

Shelley Fisher Fishkin, *Was Huck Black?: Mark Twain and African American Voices.* New York: Oxford University Press, 1993.

Hamlin Hill, *Mark Twain: God's Fool.* New York: Harper & Row, 1973.

Justin Kaplan, *Mr. Clemens and Mark Twain: A Biography.* New York: Simon & Schuster, 1966.

———, ed., *Mark Twain: A Profile*. New York: Hill and Wang, 1967.

Randall Knoper, *Acting Naturally: Mark Twain in the Culture of Performance*. Berkeley and Los Angeles: University of California Press, 1995.

J.R. LeMaster and James D. Wilson, eds., *The Mark Twain Encyclopedia*. New York: Garland, 1993.

James S. Leonard et al. eds., *Satire or Evasion: Black Perspectives on Huckleberry Finn*. Durham, NC: Duke University Press, 1992.

William R. Macnaughton, *Mark Twain's Last Years as a Writer*. Columbia: University of Missouri Press, 1979.

Bruce Michelson, *Mark Twain on the Loose: A Comic Writer and the American Self*. Amherst: University of Massachusetts Press, 1995.

Ron Powers, *Dangerous Water: A Biography of the Boy Who Became Mark Twain*. New York: BasicBooks, 1999.

Forest G. Robinson, *In Bad Faith: The Dynamics of Deception in Mark Twain's America*. Cambridge, MA: Harvard University Press, 1986.

Margaret Sanborn, *Mark Twain: The Bachelor Years*. New York: Doubleday, 1990.

Robert Sattelmeyer and J. Donald Crowley, eds., *One Hundred Years of Huckleberry Finn: The Boy, His Book, and American Culture*. Columbia: University of Missouri Press, 1985.

Jeffrey Steinbrink, *Getting to Be Mark Twain*. Berkeley and Los Angeles: University of California Press, 1991.

Edward Wagenknecht, *Mark Twain: The Man and His Work*. Norman: University of Oklahoma Press, 1967.

Resa Willis, *Mark and Livy: The Love Story of Mark Twain and the Woman Who Almost Tamed Him*. New York: Athenaeum, 1992.

INDEX